THE CIVIL WAR IN WEST VIRGINIA
A PICTORIAL HISTORY

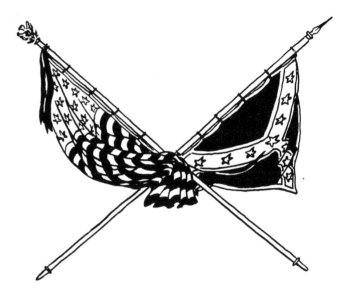

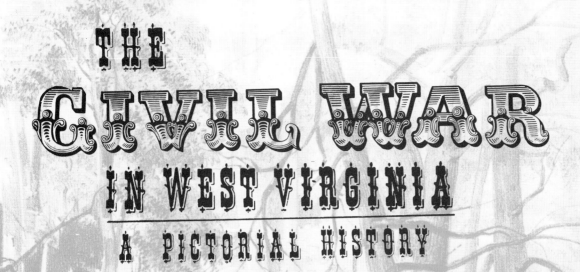

THE
GIVIL WAR
IN WEST VIRGINIA
A PICTORIAL HISTORY

BY STAN COHEN

PICTORIAL HISTORIES PUBLISHING COMPANY
CHARLESTON, WEST VIRGINIA

LIBRARY OF CONGRESS NO. 76-2880
ISBN 0-933126-02-6

First Printing 1976
Second Printing 1977
Third Printing 1979
Fourth Printing 1981
First Printing Revised Text 1982
Second Printing Revised Text 1984
Third Printing Revised Text 1985
Fourth Printing Revised Text 1987
Fifth Printing Revised Text 1991
Sixth Printing Revised Text 1992

REVISED EDITION
LIBRARY OF CONGRESS NO. 82-80964
ISBN 0-933126-17-4

Printed in Canada

COVER: *Original lithograph of the
Rich Mountain Battle. Color art by American
Print Gallery, Gettysburg, Pennsylvania*

PICTORIAL HISTORIES PUBLISHING COMPANY
4103 Virginia Ave. SE
Charleston, West Virginia 25304

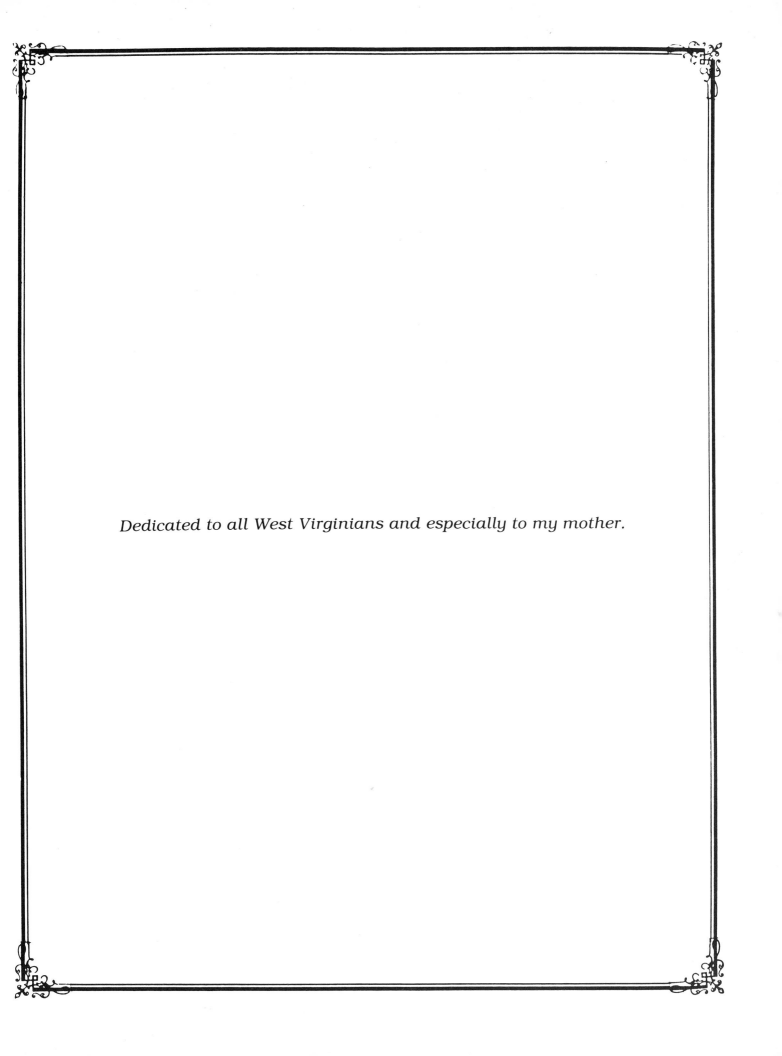

Dedicated to all West Virginians and especially to my mother.

Union soldier at Harpers Ferry. NA

Table of Contents

MAP INDEX

Foreword

One has only to travel through the West Virginia countryside to appreciate the difficulties the Civil War soldier had in waging war there. Although the state was not the scene of major battles that shaped the outcome of the war (except perhaps for Harpers Ferry in 1862), the occurrence of more than 600 minor battles, skirmishes and raids between 1861 and 1865 showed that both North and South considered West Virginia a vital piece of real estate.

It was brother against brother, neighbor against neighbor in this theater of war. The state furnished some 30,000 troops to the Union and from 7,000 to 9,000 to the Confederacy. The state was one of the highest in percentage of total population enlisting as Federal troops. These soldiers fought near their homes and in every distant zone of the war.

Many more men and a few women were in the home guards and local partisan units and some fought on neither side but used the war as an excuse for killing and stealing for their own pleasure and gain.

Maps of the period show that the state was a gateway to the Ohio River and the Midwestern states if the South had control, and to the Virginia Valley if the North held sway. The mountainous terrain precluded the mass troop movements characteristic of the other theaters.

The deciding factor for both sides to consider, and it had a lot to do with the formation of West Virginia as a political entity, was the existence of two railroads: the Baltimore and Ohio in the northern part of the state, and the Virginia and Tennessee just over the border in Virginia in the south. These railroads were the lifeblood of both sides.

Since the state was a buffer between north and south, the first military actions of the war occurred here. And there were other firsts of the Civil War (and in some instances of modern warfare) such as: the military use of telegraph, indirect artillery fire, first Union and Confederate soldiers killed, first general killed and an oil field destroyed.

I have tried in this book to trace the highlights of the war through pictures of sites as they look now and as they looked then. Time and people have not been kind to many sites. Nevertheless, much of the past remains. I hope this book will give the West Virginian and the Civil War buff from outside the state a closer picture of events that shaped the state's history. There are many good books available to the reader who wants to explore events in more detail.

I wish to thank the following for making this book possible: Bill McNeel of the Pocahontas Times in Marlinton; Walter Leach, superintendent of Carnifex Ferry Battlefield State Park; Miss Genevieve Smith of Beverly; Miss Mary Jenkins, librarian at the State Archives in Charleston; Bruce Graham of S. Spencer Moore Company in Charleston; Bob Hart of Belington; Tom Ryan of Fayetteville; R.H. Bowman of Rainelle; Rodney Pyles and Golda Riggs of the West Virginia University Library Archives; Mrs. G. Roderick Cheesman of Boydville in Martinsburg; Jack Zinn of Nutter Fork; Mrs. Beverly Fluty of Wheeling; and Barbara McCallum and Bob McGiffert who edited my manuscript.

FOREWORD TO REVISED EDITION

I published the first edition of this book in 1976 for the Bicentennial year. It has subsequently gone through three reprintings. Since that time I have continued to research the subject and hunt for drawings and photographs which were overlooked or undiscovered.

Many people have sent me comments on different aspects of the West Virginia campaign, and many have shed new light on the narrative and photographs included in my earlier book. With the wealth of new information, photographs and maps made available in the ensuing years, I decided to expand the book, add to the narrative and correct some of the discrepancies. I believe that this revised edition contains the most complete pictorial documentation of the war as it was fought in West Virginia. This book does not attempt to go into detail on every campaign that took place in the four-year period; there are many books available for the person who wants to study the actions in detail.

Photographing the campaign in West Virginia was an uncommon occupation. The rugged terrain made it difficult to transport the heavy, cumbersome photographic paraphernalia of the day, and campaigns were usually short and engagements small. Besides this, much of the action consisted of guerrilla activity, which, naturally, did not lend itself to photographic purposes.

Yet there is an amazing amount of material available if one digs deeply enough. There are a prolific number of lithographic drawings available, especially of the early actions.

I would like to thank all the people who helped me put together the revised edition, the people who offered a casual remark or tidbit about one particular encounter as well as the people who took the time to write to me. Especially helpful was Terry Lowry of South Charleston who provided some of the new 1861 material and who has written the definitive work on the early Kanawha Valley Campaign and the Scary Creek Battle. Jack Smith of Salem also helped with his lengthy account of the Buffington Island engagement, as did Mrs. Ruth Elmore of Athens, W. Va. who provided an account of the Piegon's Roost engagement in Mercer County.

The success of this book, the first of fifteen that I've written to date, leads me to believe that West Virginians are deeply interested in the events and aware of the struggles that led to the formation of the state.

Stan Cohen
April 1982

Photo Credits

The photographs and drawings in this book are from a variety of sources. The new photographs with no acknowledgement were taken by the author in the past ten years. Many others list their source.

The excellent lithographs originally done on stone by Corp. J. Nep. Roesler of Color Guard, Co. G, 47th Regiment, Ohio Volunteers, are from the West Virginia State Archives. They were sketched on duty in Nicholas and Fayette Counties in 1861, lithographed in Cincinnati, and sold during and after the war. Roesler did 23 drawings in all and left an excellent visual record of early military life in the southcentral part of the state.

The rest of the photographs and drawings are credited to these sources:

WVU Archives - Morgantown
W. Va. State Archives - Charleston
Terry Lowry - South Charleston
HFNHP - Harpers Ferry National Historical Park
Virginia State Archives - Richmond
Chessie System, B and O Archives - Baltimore, Md.
HPU - Historic Preservation Unit, Charleston
USAMHI - United States Army Military History Institute, Carlisle, Pa.
NA - National Archives, Washington, D.C.
RBHL - Rutherford B. Hayes Library, Fremont, Ohio
Gary Bays - Charleston

A vivid portrayal of irregulars, partisans or guerrilla fighters for the South in the mountains of West Virginia.
WVU Archives

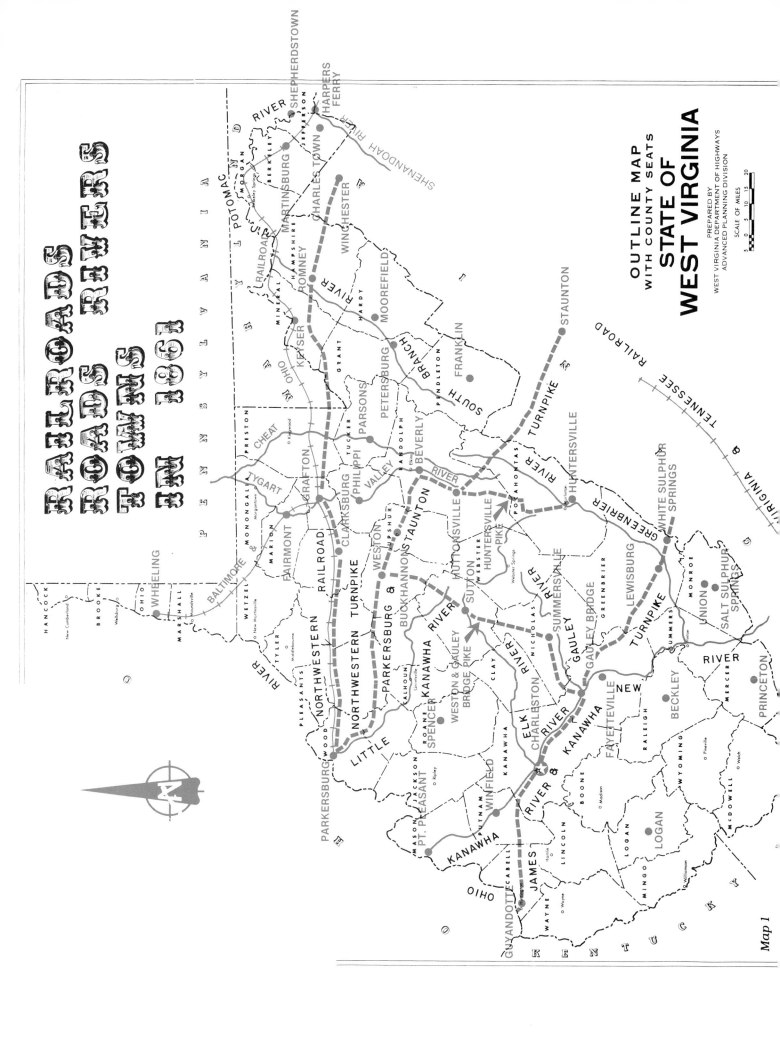

RAILROADS
ROADS
TOWNS
IN 1861

OUTLINE MAP
WITH COUNTY SEATS
STATE OF
WEST VIRGINIA

PREPARED BY
WEST VIRGINIA DEPARTMENT OF HIGHWAYS
ADVANCED PLANNING DIVISION

SCALE OF MILES
5 0 5 10 15 20

Map 1

Prelude To War

Although it preceded the Civil War by a year and a half, John Brown's raid on the U.S. Arsenal at Harpers Ferry, Jefferson County on Oct. 16, 1859, helped shape the war's events in the following years.

Brown, a long-time advocate of abolition, wanted to arm the slaves and promote a general uprising in the South. He had received his baptism of fire in "Bleeding Kansas" in the late 1850s when he gained national notoriety as a bold and ruthless leader.

The anti-slavery movement so engrossed him that he once stated: "I have only a short time to live —only one death to die, and I will die fighting for this cause. There will be no more peace in this land until slavery is done for. I will give them something else to do than to extend slave territory. I will carry this war into Africa." His words were to come true only too shortly.

He was determined to occupy a stronghold in a mountainous area in or near a slave state from whence he could promote an uprising and defend himself against attack. Harpers Ferry was chosen as the spot, and he gathered a band of dedicated followers around him.

A base of operations was established on a farm a few miles away in Maryland, and supplies and arms were assembled for the impending attack on the arsenal. He had gathered over 1,000 long pikes to arm the slaves that he expected and hoped would rush to his side once he had captured Harpers Ferry.

By mid-October, Brown had recruited only 21 men, but he decided he could wait no longer and picked the night of October 16 for the attack.

After reaching the B and O Railroad bridge at the Potomac River and capturing the watchman, he seized the arsenal without firing a shot. Brown sent several raiders on a special mission to capture Col. Lewis W. Washington, the 46-year-old great grand-nephew of George Washington. He lived at "Beall-air," five miles west of Harpers Ferry and owned a pistol and sword that had belonged to the first President. Brown wanted these weapons for himself.

Several other civilians were taken, but at 1:25 a.m. the first note of alarm was sounded. A train was allowed to pass through town on the way to Baltimore and the word spread throughout the country.

Militia units were called out, and citizens of Harpers Ferry gathered arms. Brown had been urged to flee, but he resisted and now it was too late. The trap was sprung, the town was sealed off, and most of the remaining invaders and hostages sought refuge in the fire enginehouse at the armory's entrance.

By nightfall the entire area was in an uproar. The Federal government sent Lt. Col. Robert E. Lee with a force of U.S. Marines, the only force immediately available, to crush the rebellion. Lee had as his lieutenant Jeb Stuart, who was later to become Lee's cavalry commander.

Several times, Brown was asked to surrender, but he refused. On the morning of the 18th, the Marines stormed the enginehouse, and after a brief skirmish, captured him and freed the hostages. Brown was seriously wounded, but upon his capture issued a prophetic warning: "I wish to say furthermore, that you had better—all you people in the South—prepare yourselves for a settlement of that question that must come up for settlement sooner

John Brown (1800-59).   HFNHP

-1-

than you are prepared for it. The sooner you are prepared the better. You may dispose of me very easily; I am nearly disposed of now; but this question is still to be settled – this negro question I mean – the end of that is not yet."

The day after their capture, Brown and his four surviving followers were taken to the county jail in Charles Town. A treason trial began on October 25 and Brown was found guilty and sentenced to hang. The sentence was carried out on Dec. 2, 1859, not far from the courthouse.

T.J. Jackson (later to be known as "Stonewall" Jackson) attended the hanging with a troop from the Virginia Military Institute. A trooper named John Wilkes Booth was another witness, as was Edmund Ruffin, an arch-secessionist from Virginia who supposedly fired the first shot of the war at Fort Sumter.

Although Brown did not succeed in his scheme to free the slaves, he became a martyr for the abolition cause in the North, and three years later, on Jan.1, 1863, the slaves were freed by President Lincoln.

Jefferson County Courthouse, where John Brown was tried for treason, as it looks today. Erected in 1836 at the corner of North George and East Washington Streets, Charles Town, it was remodeled in 1871-72. During the war it served as a Union Army barracks. It was damaged by shell fire and all the county records were removed to Lexington, Va. The leaders of the Miners' Armed March on Logan County in 1921 were also tried here for treason.   State of West Virginia

U.S. Marines storming the enginehouse on Oct. 18, 1859 under the command of Lt. Col. Robert E. Lee.

John Brown's fort at Harpers Ferry, Jefferson County. It was built in 1848 to house the fire engines and watchmen for the armory. It originally stood at the entrance gates to the Armory where the train station now stands. It was torn down in 1893 and shipped to the Chicago Worlds Fair. An individual purchased it and rebuilt it at Harpers Ferry. In 1909, Storer College acquired it and moved it to the college campus on the heights above town. The National Park Service moved it back to its present site and restored it.

Street scene, Charlestown, during trial of John Brown, showing Jail and Court House

JAIL

COURT HOUSE

COPYRIGHT 1908, BY W.L. ERWIN

Street scene in Charles Town during the trial. Author's collection.

John Brown's Fort in the 1890s. NA

-4-

Brown is shown riding on his coffin from the Charles Town jail to his execution site.   HFNHP

The original wagon is now on display at the Jefferson County Museum in Charles Town. The wagon was drawn by two white horses. The sheriff and jailer walked in front and were flanked by three companies of infantry.
                                                                    Jefferson County Museum

Brown was executed at 11:30 a.m. on Dec. 2, 1859, in a field just outside Charles Town, Jefferson County.
HFNHP

Beallair, the home of Col. Lewis W. Washington, located on CR 24, near Halltown, Jefferson County. The original part of the house was built by Thomas Beall before 1800. It passed out of the Washington family in 1877 and fell into disrepair.
Ed Fitzpatrick: Charles Town, W. Va.

A Call to Arms, Secession, Restoration and Statehood

The firing on Fort Sumter and President Lincoln's call to arms in April 1861 set Virginia on the road to secession from the Union and membership in the Confederacy. A convention in Richmond passed a secession ordinance on April 17, 1861, and ordered it put to a vote of the people. The delegates and people of the western counties overwhelmingly voted against the ordinance and talked of leaving the mother state.

For the most part the people of the western 34 counties of Virginia had always felt apart from their eastern brothers because of the lack of money and support from the Richmond government, the differences in terrain between the two sections and the absence of slave labor in the west.

The *Wheeling Intelligencer*, which was started in 1852 and was edited by the brilliant statesman, A.W. Campbell, was an early advocate of statehood and the only newspaper in Virginia to support Lincoln for President in 1860. It asked in one of its issues, "If Virginia can secede from the United States, why cannot West Virginia secede from Virginia?"

After the secession ordinance was passed, the western delegates came home and mass meetings were held throughout the region to denounce the action taken at Richmond. At the First Wheeling Convention on May 13 the foundation for statehood was laid. The Second Wheeling Convention convened on June 11 with 57 delegates in attendance. A "Restored Government of Virginia" was established with Francis H. Pierpont as the first governor. The congressmen from the "restored state" were seated in Congress, and President Lincoln recognized them. This secession from another state without that state's permission is unparalleled in American history and has been questioned for constitutional legality.

The Second Wheeling Convention adopted on June 17, 1861, the following "Declaration of the People of Virginia" which is one of the most important state papers in West Virginia history:

THE TRUE PURPOSE OF ALL GOVERNMENT is to promote the welfare and provide for the protection and security of the governed, and when any form or organization of government proves inadequate for, or subversive of this purpose, it is the right , it is the duty of the latter to abolish it. The Bill of Rights of Virginia, framed in 1776, re-affirmed in 1830, and again in 1851, express-

ly reserves this right to a majority of her people. The act of the General Assembly, calling the Convention which assembled in Richmond in February last, without the previously expressed consent of such majority, was therefore a usurpation; and the Convention thus called has not only abused the powers nominally entrusted to it, but, with the connivance and active aid of the executive, has usurped and exercised other powers, to the manifest injury of the people, which, if permitted, will inevitably subject them to a military despotism.

UNION OR DISUNION?

THE ISSUE IS UPON US!

As meetings are being held in portions of our State urging a call for a convention to consider whether Virginia shall unite with South Carolina and the Cotton States in their treasonable efforts to dissolve the Union of these States, it is deemed advisable that the citizens of Harrison county give expression to their sentiments in mass-meeting assembled.

It is the settled conviction of intelligent observers of the times that the Union, formed by our fathers and cemented with their blood---a Union hallowed by all the sacred memories of the past, and endeared to us by the innumerable blessings of the present---is seriously threatened. Even now our monetary interests and business relations have received a shock from the impending destruction of our Government little less disastrous than war itself. The credit of both States and individuals is not only being destroyed, but ruin begins to stare us in the face. Shall Virginia be a participant in this effort at self-destruction? Will she, too, be guilty of self-murder? It is for her People to say. Rely upon it, the time is now come when, if we would avert the horrid calamities of civil war, the people of Harrison should give unmistakable utterance of their devotion to the National Union, and their unalterable attachment and unyielding determination to preserve, unimpaired, the glorious Constitution of the American Confederacy. MARK IT WELL, your silence will be mistaken for indifference, and will tend to strengthen the traitorous hands already stretched forth to destroy the Government. It is of the utmost consequence, then, that the voice of the people be heard, trumpet-tongued, commanding peace. Let every man who values this Government and is opposed to treason, leave his farm, his work-shop, his store, and his counting-room, and give one day to his Country. Do this, we earnestly beseech you, before it is too late. Let no man, therefore, neglect this patriotic call, remembering that he who is not for the Union is against it. Come, then, citizens of Harrison county, to the

MASS-MEETING,

To be held at the Court-house, in Clarksburg, on Saturday next,

The 24th of November, 1860.

Come prepared to resist any and every attempt to sunder the tie which binds us together, and which has hitherto united us as one people.

Clarksburg, Va., November 20th, 1860.

This broadside issued in Clarksburg, Harrison County in November 1860 is an indication of how strong the sentiment was for preserving the Union in the northern part of western Virginia.
WVU Archives

The Convention, by its pretended ordinances, has required the people of Virginia to separate from and wage war against the government of the United States, and against citizens of neighboring States, with whom they have heretofore maintained friendly, social and business relations:

It has attempted to subvert the Union founded by Washington and his co-patriots, in the purer days of the republic, which has conferred unexampled prosperity upon every class of citizens, and upon every section of the country:

It has been attempted to transfer the allegiance of the people to an illegal confederacy of rebellious States, and required their submission to its pretended edicts and decrees:

It has attempted to place the whole military force and military operations of the Commonwealth under the control and direction of such confederacy, for offensive as well as defensive purposes:

It has, in conjunction with the State executive, instituted wherever their usurped power extends, a reign of terror intended to suppress the free expression of the will of the people, making elections a mockery and a fraud.

The same combination, even before the passage of the pretended ordinance of secession, instituted war by the seizure and appropriation of the property of the Federal Government, and by organizing and mobilizing armies, with the avowed purpose of capturing or destroying the Capital of the Union:

They have attempted to bring the allegiance of the people of the United States into direct conflict with their subordinate allegiance to the State, thereby making obedience to their pretended Ordinances, treason against the former.

We, therefore, the delegates here assembled in Convention to devise such measures and take such action as the safety and welfare of the loyal citizens of Virginia may demand, having maturely considered the premises, and viewing with great concern the deplorable condition to which this once happy Commonwealth must be reduced unless some regular adequate remedy is speedily adopted, and appealing to the Supreme Ruler of the Universe for the rectitude of our intentions, do hereby, in the name and on the behalf of the good people of Virginia, solemnly declare, that the preservation of their dearest rights and liberties and their security in person and property, imperatively demand the reorganization of the government of the Commonwealth, and that all acts of said Convention and Executive, tending to separate this Commonwealth from the United States, or to levy and carry on war against them, are without authority and void; and that the offices of all who adhere to the said Convention and Executive, whether legislative, executive or judicial, are vacated.

The "Restored Government of Virginia" gave its blessing to the formation of a new state and the first constitution was completed on Feb. 18, 1862. On April 3, 1862, the Constitution was ratified by a vote of 18,862 to 514 after some changes had been made in the provisions on slavery. On Dec. 31, 1862, President Lincoln signed a bill authorizing the admission of the new state of West Virginia, which at first was to be called Kanawha. On April 20, 1863, Lincoln issued a proclamation granting statehood effective June 20, 1863. The capital was established at Wheeling and Arthur I. Boreman was elected the first governor.

Thirty-nine counties were included in the proposed state after Pocahontas, Greenbrier, Monroe, Mercer and McDowell were added to get more counties with Democratic party majorities. The Republicans did not want any former Virginia slave counties in the state, but accepted these five because the mountains in the counties gave the new state a natural barrier. The eastern panhandle counties of Pendleton, Hardy, Hampshire, Berkeley, Jefferson and Morgan, were included for protection and because of the fact that the Baltimore and Ohio Railroad wanted all of its track included in the new state's boundaries.

The last had not been heard, however, from the mother state of Virginia. She sued West Virginia in 1906 for debts unpaid after the new state took over property (the State Hospital at Weston and a few roads) on June 20, 1863. The compensation amounted to more than four million dollars in principal and more than eight million in interest. West Virginia acknowledged the debt, but final payment was not made until July 1, 1939.

Virginians loyal to the Union met in June 1861, in the third floor courtroom of the Custom House to demand a "restored" government of Virginia. The July 6, 1861 edition of Harper's Weekly *depicted the scene.*

W. Va. Independence Hall Foundation

Another view of Independence Hall, also known as the Custom House, 1861.

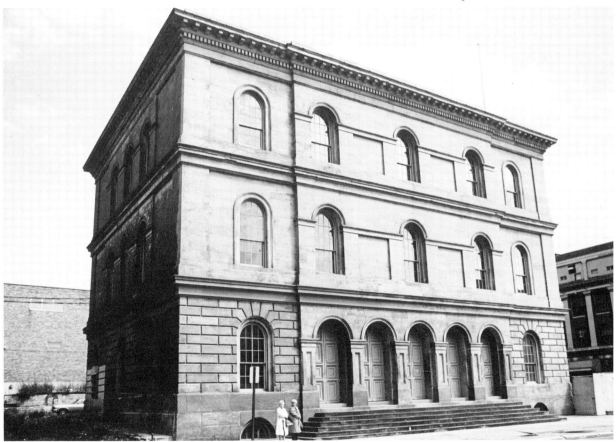

Independence Hall, Wheeling, Ohio County, site of the birth of West Virginia. It was here in 1861, that the "Declaration of Rights" was adopted and the Restored Government of Virginia was established. The building was erected in 1859 at the corner of Market and 16th streets and has been restored by the West Virginia Independence Hall Foundation.

State of West Virginia

Arthur I. Boreman (1823-96). A resident of Tyler County, a lawyer and member of the Virginia Assembly, he presided over the Second Wheeling Convention in June 1861 and was elected first governor of the new state of West Virginia. He took office on June 20, 1863 and served until 1869. He was then elected to the United States Senate, later practiced law in Parkersburg and was appointed a judge in 1888.   WVU Archives

Francis H. Pierpont (1814-99). He was a lawyer from Monongalia County and a leader in the formation of the new state of West Virginia. His plan was used to set up the Restored Government of Virginia and he was elected its governor at the Second Wheeling Convention in June 1861. After the new state was admitted to the Union, the government was moved to Alexandria, Virginia, and then to Richmond at the end of the war. He was removed from office in 1867 because he was accused of being too conciliatory to the State of Virginia.

W. Va. State Archives

Store front at 1406 Main Street, Wheeling, before and after June 20, 1863.

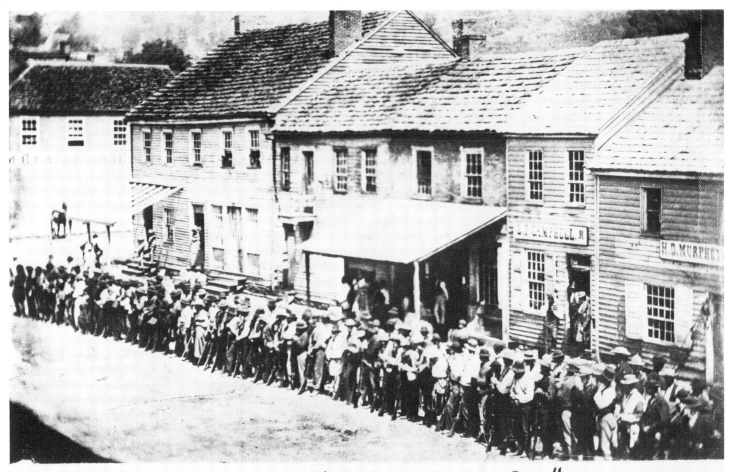

_ARRICO CORNER -- HIGH & WALNUT STS. 1861-"CALL TO ARMS.

Union volunteers assembled at the corner of High and Walnut Streets in Morgantown, Monongalia County in 1861. WVU Archives

1,010 BRAVE MEN WANTED!

I am authorized by Governor Pierpoint to raise a Regiment of men to consist of

TEN COMPANIES

of 101 men each, including officers. When two companies are formed they will be mustered into service and a camp will be established at or near Morgantown, where they will be armed, equipped and drilled until the Regiment is full and ordered into service.

July 29, 1861.   JAMES EVANS.

Broadside issued for recruits to join the Union Army in northern West Virginia.
W.Va. State Archives

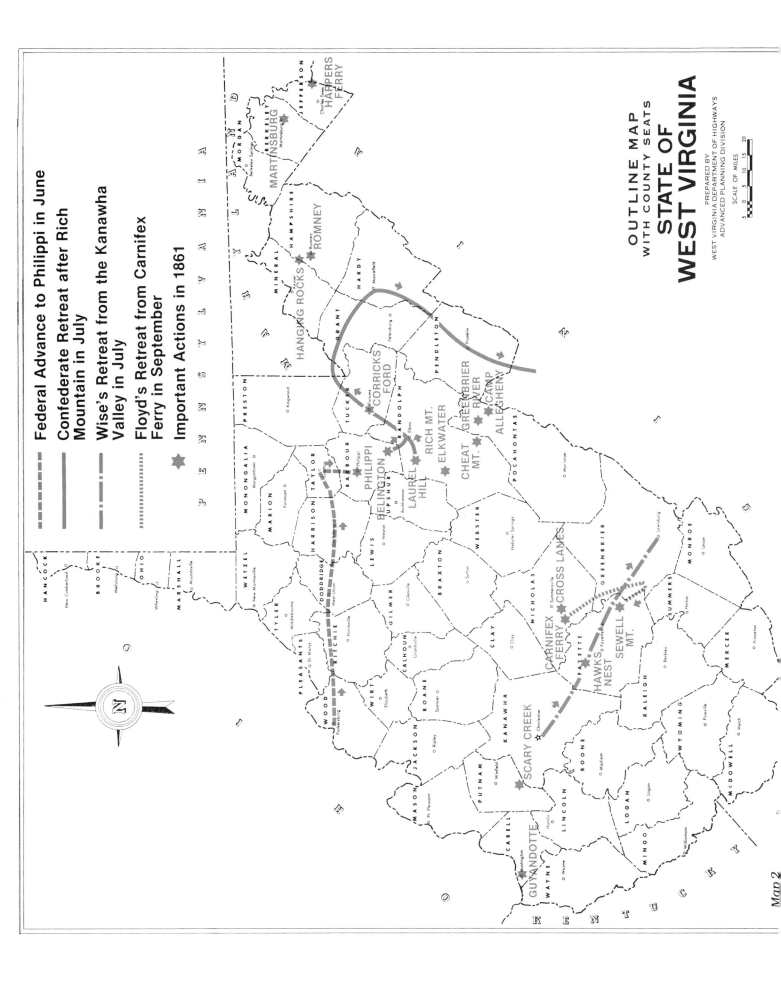

OUTLINE MAP
WITH COUNTY SEATS
STATE OF
WEST VIRGINIA

PREPARED BY
WEST VIRGINIA DEPARTMENT OF HIGHWAYS
ADVANCED PLANNING DIVISION

SCALE OF MILES
5 0 5 10 15 20

Federal Advance to Philippi in June

Confederate Retreat after Rich Mountain in July

Wise's Retreat from the Kanawha Valley in July

Floyd's Retreat from Carnifex Ferry in September

★ **Important Actions in 1861**

Map 2

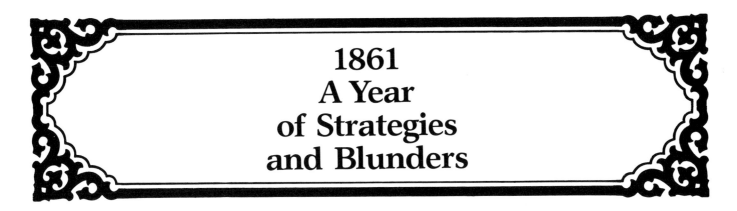

1861
A Year
of Strategies
and Blunders

A map of western Virginia in 1861 would show four transportation routes through the region to the northern states: the James River and Kanawha Turnpike through the Great Kanawha Valley, the Parkersburg and Staunton Turnpike through the center of the state, the Northwestern Pike following the line of present-day Route 50 and the Baltimore and Ohio Railroad in the north. These areas were fought over in 1861, and almost every action throughout the war was directly connected to one of these routes.

The governor of Virginia, John Letcher, issued two proclamations to the people of northwestern Virginia on June 14, 1861. In the first he announced adoption of the Ordinance of Secession by the Virginia voters at the election on May 23 and also proclaimed the constitution of the Provisional Government of the Confederate States of America in force throughout Virginia.

His second proclamation, which follows, appealed directly to the people of the northwest where the restoration of the Virginia government was underway at Wheeling. It was published at Huttonsville, Randolph County, and circulated in counties occupied by Southern forces:

THE SOVEREIGN PEOPLE OF VIRGINIA unbiased and by their own free choice have by a majority of nearly one hundred thousand qualified voters, severed the ties that heretofore bound them to the government of the United States, and united this Commonwealth with the Confederate States....

The State of Virginia has now the second time in her history asserted this right, and it is the duty of every Virginian to acknowledge her act when ratified by such majority, and to his willing co-operation to make good the declaration. All her people have voted, each has taken his chance to have his personal views represented.

You as well as the rest of the State have cast your vote fairly and the majority is against you. It is the duty of good citizens to yield to the will of the State. The bill of rights has proclaimed "that the people have a right to uniform government, and that, therefore, no government separate from or independent of the government of Virginia ought to be erected or established within the limits thereof." The majority thus declared therefore have a right to govern.

But notwithstanding this right that exercise has been regarded by the people of all sections of the United States, as undoubted, and sacred, yet the government at Washington now utterly denies it, and by the exercise of despotic power is endeavoring to coerce our people to abject submission to their authority. Virginia has asserted her independence. She will maintain it at every hazard. She is sustained by the power of her sister Southern States, ready and willing to uphold her cause. Can any true Virginian refuse to render assistance?

TO THE PEOPLE
Of the Department of the KANAWHA VALLEY, embracing the following Counties, viz: Mason, Jackson, Putnam, Cabell, Wayne, Logan, Kanawha, Boone, Wyoming, Raleigh, Fayette, Nicholas and Clay: According to the following order, by the

Governor of Virginia:
Executive Department, April 29, 1861.

LIEUT. COL. McCAUSLAND:

Sir: You will proceed at once to the Kanawha Valley and assume command of the volunteer forces in that section, and organize and muster the same into the service of the State; and as soon as they are formed into Battalions or Regiments, report the fact to me, with the names of the company officers, the number of men in each company, and the kind and quality of arms.

Gen. Lee will give all necessary orders for your government in that command.   I am very respectfully,
JOHN LETCHER.

I have arrived here to take command of the Department. I have instructions to call into the field ten companies, and one company of artillery. These troops will be encamped in the Kanawha Valley, near Buffalo, Putnam Co. They are intended for the protection of the Department; and I appeal to the people of the border counties to abstain from anything which will arouse ill feeling on either side of the Ohio river. This Department is organized by the proper authority in the State, and is provided with the credit to sustain itself; but for complete success, I firmly rely on the friendly disposition of the people therein.

The volunteer companies of the counties of Mason, Jackson and Putnam, will rendezvous at BUFFALO, Putnam Co.

The volunteer companies of the counties of Cabell, Wayne, and Logan, will rendezvous at BARBOURSVILLE, Cabell county.

The volunteer companies of the counties of Kanawha, Boone, Wyoming, Raleigh, Fayette, Nicholas and Clay, will rendezvous at CHARLESTON, Kanawha county.

The Captain of the volunteer companies in the above counties will remain at their respective drill grounds, until ordered to their rendezvous by the Commandant of the Department. So soon as preparation to receive them can be made, the companies will be ordered to their respective rendezvous, mustered into the service of the State, and then ordered to the Camp of Instruction. No company will be mustered into service unless it has at least 82 men.

The Captains will see that each man is provided with a uniform, one blanket, one haversack, one extra pair of shoes, two flannel shirts (to be worn in the place of the ordinary shirts), two pairs of drawers, four pairs of woolen socks, four handkerchiefs, towels, one comb and brush and tooth-brush, two pairs white gloves, one pair of rough pantaloons for fatigue duty, needles, thread, wax, buttons, &c., in a small buckskin bag. The whole (excepting the blanket) will be placed in a bag, this bag will be placed on the blanket and rolled up, and be secured to the back of each man by two straps.

Lt. Col. JNO. McCAUSLAND,
Commanding Dep't Ka. Valley.

Broadside issued by Lt. Col. John McCausland on orders of Gov. John Letcher of Virginia to recruit troops for state service.   W. Va. State Archives

McCLELLAN TAKES COMMAND

Union men, alarmed at the southern occupation of the Kanawha Valley and the railroad junction at Grafton, Taylor County, sent an appeal to Gen. George McClellan, commander of the Department of Ohio, for assistance in protecting the railroad and the Union people in the area. McClellan hesitated to send troops, thinking the people would consider them invaders, but on May 1, 1861, he sent soldiers to Parkersburg, Benwood and Wheeling. He issued a proclamation on May 26:

> "To the Union Men of Western Virginia.
> Virginians:"
>
> The general government has long enough endured the machinations of a few factious rebels in your midst. Armed traitors have in vain endeavored to deter you from expressing your loyalty at the polls. Having failed in their infamous attempts to deprive you of the exercise of your dearest rights, they now seek to inaugurate a reign of terror and thus force you to yield to their schemes and submit to the yoke of the Southern Confederacy. They are destroying the property of Citizens, and ruining your magnificent railroads. The general Government has hithertofore carefully abstained from sending troops across the Ohio, or even posting them along the banks, although frequently urged to do so by many of your prominent citizens. I determined to wait the result of the late election, desirous that no one might be able to say that the slightest effort has been made from this side to influence you in the free expression of your opinion, although many agencies were brought to bear upon you by the rebels were well known.
>
> "You have shown under adverse circumstances, that the great mass of the people of Western Virginia are true and loyal to the beneficent government under which we and our fathers have lived so long. As soon as the result of the election was known the traitors commenced their works of destruction. The general Government cannot close its ears or eyes to the demand you have made for assistance. I have ordered troops to cross the river. They come to you as friends and brothers, as enemies to the armed rebels who are preying on you. Your homes, your families and your property are safe under their protection. All your rights shall be religiously respected.
>
> "Notwithstanding all that has been said by the traitors to induce you to believe that our advent among you will be signalized by interference with your slaves, understand one thing clearly, not only will we abstain from such interference but we will crush any attempt at insurrection with an iron hand.
>
> "Now that we are in your midst, I call upon you to fly to arms and support the general government, sever the connection that bind you to traitors. Proclaim to the world that faith and loyalty so long boasted by the Old Dominion is still preserved in Western Virginia and that you remain true to the stars and stripes."

On the same day McClellan addressed the soldiers who were to comprise the expedition into western Virginia:

> "SOLDIERS:" You are ordered to cross the frontier and enter upon the soil of Virginia. Your mission is to restore peace and confidence, to protect the majesty of the law and to rescue our brethern from the grasp of armed traitors. You are to act in concert with the Virginia troops and support their advance. I place under the protection of your honor, the persons and property of the Virginians. I know that you will respect their feelings and their rights. Preserve the strictest discipline, remember that each one of you holds the honor of Ohio and the Union in your keeping.
>
> "If you are called upon to overcome armed opposition I know that your courage is equal to the task, but remember that your only foes are the armed traitors, and show mercy to them when they are in your power, for many are misled. When under your protection the loyal men of Western Virginia have been enabled to organize and they can protect themselves, and then you can return to your homes with the proud satisfaction of having preserved a gallant people from destruction."

McClellan arrived at Parkersburg on June 21 knowing that he had a large force of over 20,000 men to counter any Confederate move. He had stationed along the B & O Railroad, 27 regiments of infantry, four batteries of six guns each and two troops of cavalry.

Gen. George B. McClellan (1826-85). Commander of Ohio troops at the beginning of the war and of Union troops in West Virginia until July 22, 1861, when he was called to Washington to assume overall command of the Union army.
WVU Archives

Parkersburg, Wood County, in 1861 was the terminus of the Northwestern branch of the Baltimore and Ohio Railroad and the Northwestern Turnpike and was an important embarkation point for Federal troops coming into western Virginia.   Author's Collection

General Rosecrans and staff at his headquarters in Clarksburg, Harrison County in June 1861. Clarksburg was an important supply depot for Union forces in the northern part of the state.

West Virginia Hillbilly

B & O RAILROAD

The most important route through the state was the Baltimore and Ohio Railroad, which ran from Washington, D.C. and Baltimore through Maryland, entered West Virginia at Harpers Ferry, and continued on to Wheeling and Parkersburg. It was the only through line from Washington to Cincinnati and St. Louis.

The railroad had been built to Harpers Ferry in 1834, to Piedmont in 1851, to Fairmont in 1852 and Wheeling in 1853. A branch line, the Northwestern Railroad from Grafton to Parkersburg had been finished in 1857. The route traveled some of the most remote and rugged terrain in the east and at the time was an engineering marvel.

Its tracks carried the troops and supplies for the eastern and western theaters of war. The railroad was the cause of frequent battles, raids and skirmishes and its protection tied up thousands of Union troops all along its line.

Whichever side controlled the railroad would have a convenient conduit to the other's territory. At first, railroad officials tried to remain neutral, but when Maryland decided to stay in the Union, the company sought protection from Federal troops as the route now passed through distinctly rebel territory, especially in the eastern counties of western Virginia.

Soon after the Virginia Ordinance of Secession was passed, Southern Col. T.J. (later Stonewall) Jackson captured Harpers Ferry and sought to control the railroad. He found that the night trains that passed through town disturbed his sleep and ordered the president of the line to alter the schedules. By changing the schedules Jackson was able to block the line from Point of Rocks, twelve miles east of Harpers Ferry, to a point just west of Martinsburg, thus trapping more than 50 locomotives and 300 freight cars in between. These freight cars were hauling coal from Cumberland, Md. to Baltimore for use by the Union ships blockading southern ports. This of course could not be tolerated.

It was soon decided however that Harpers Ferry was an indefensible position for the Confederates, and so on June 14 they destroyed the railroad bridge across the Potomac River and evacuated the town. Jackson was ordered to destroy all the trapped rolling stock and the railroad buildings at Martinsburg to prevent their use by Union forces. He had the cars and buildings burned, but, follow-

Grafton, Taylor County in 1861. The town was a very important railroad junction on the Baltimore and Ohio mainline to Wheeling, Parkersburg and Gen. McClellan's headquarters in 1861.

Valley House.   B. & O. R. R. Machine Shop and Track.   Grafton House.   North-Wes

NO. 121.—VIEW OF GRAFTON, WESTERN VIRGINIA, NOW OCCUPIED BY THE

The hotel and station in Grafton, Taylor County in 1861. The B & O mainline is on the right, the Northwestern branchline on the left.
                                                                                    B & O Railroad Archives

ad Bridge.   Taggart's Valley River.   Fifteenth Ohio Regiment.   Sixteenth Ohio Regiment

S TROOPS UNDER THE COMMAND OF MAJOR-GENERAL G. B. McCLELLAN.

ing his own dictates, he saved four locomotives near Harpers Ferry and ten at Martinsburg. These he sent by rail to Winchester and there had them dismantled, shipped overland to Strasburg, Va., and put to use for the South. The remainder of the rolling stock, 42 locomotives and 300 freight cars were destroyed.

This action represented the largest capture and destruction of railroad equipment during the entire war. A few days later Jackson wrote to his wife: "It was a sad work; but I had my orders and my duty was to obey. If the cost of the property could have been spent disseminating the gospel of the Prince of Peace, how much good might have been expended!"

In September 1863, the first mass movement of troops by rail occurred when 20,000 Union soldiers were detached from the eastern armies and sent to eastern Tennessee to strengthen the defenses there. They traveled through West Virginia to Wheeling on the Baltimore and Ohio Railroad. It took seven to eleven days to complete the transfer using every available engine and car on the railroad.

Locomotives that were destroyed by Jackson's troops at Martinsburg, Berkeley County in June 1861.
Berkeley-Martinsburg Public Library

Rebel troops arriving and departing from Martinsburg in early 1861. Berkeley-Martinsburg Public Library

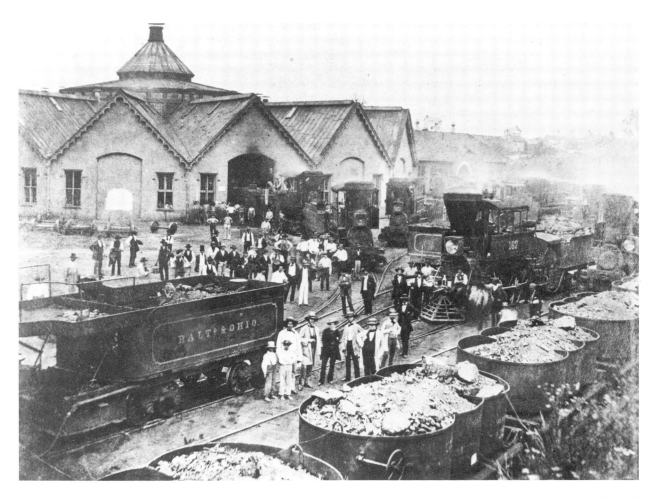

The Baltimore and Ohio Roundhouse in Martinsburg, Berkeley County, in 1860. Several Winans "Camelback" engines and three-pot gondolas are shown. Much railroad equipment and shop machinery was removed from here and sent south by Col. Jackson.   B & O Railroad Archives

These roundhouses at Martinsburg were built after the war to replace the ones burned by the Confederates in June 1861. In 1989 one was destroyed by fire.

A Winans eight-wheel "Camelback" locomotive at Martinsburg in 1860.   B & O Railroad Archives

Original Baltimore and Ohio Railroad hotel at Martinsburg, Berkeley County, built in 1849. It was not burned by Jackson on June 20, 1861 when he destroyed the shops and roundhouses across from the hotel.

The Tray Run Viaduct on the mainline of the Baltimore and Ohio Railroad near Rowlesburg, Preston County. This was one of the most important sections of the railroad and was heavily guarded by Union troops throughout the war.

Author's Collection

Two of the original piers of the Tray Run Viaduct built in 1852. It was built of cast iron, 600 feet long and 50 feet above the stone pillars. It was the largest railroad viaduct in the world at the time of construction. A new one was built in 1904.

FIRST UNION CASUALTY

Pvt. Thornsberry Bailey Brown, killed at Fetterman, Taylor County, was the first Union soldier fatality of the war.

On the night of May 22, 1861, Lt. Daniel Wilson and Pvt. Brown were ordered to Fetterman to inspect the force and position of the enemy. At the point where the tracks of the Baltimore and Ohio Railroad crossed the Northwestern Turnpike, Lt. Wilson encountered the enemy's pickets, who called him to halt. Wilson ordered Brown to fire on the enemy, and Brown's shot nicked one of the pickets in the ear. A moment later Brown fell mortally wounded with three breast wounds. Thus he was the first enlisted soldier in the United States to give up his life in the Civil War, to the organized force of the Confederates.

A monument to the memory of Thornsberry Bailey Brown was erected on May 22, 1928, at the point where Brown lost his life. The monument was moved to a spot on U.S. Route 50 and stands by the highway just west of the bridge across the Tygart Valley River.

Pvt. Brown was first interred in a cemetery near Flemington. In 1903, the Grand Army of the Republic of Grafton was granted permission by the relatives of Brown, to exhume his remains and the body was brought to Grafton and interred in the National Cemetery.

Wilson and Brown were members of the so-called "Grafton Guards," who became Company B of the Second West Virginia Infantry Volunteers. The Confederate pickets were members of Letcher's Guards.

Gen. John McCausland (1836-1927), of Mason County, who raised Confederate troops in the Kanawha Valley in the early months of the war. He fought with Gen. Floyd in his 1861 campaign and appeared in West Virginia throughout the war. He refused to surrender at Appomattox, and spent the next two years travelling in Europe and Mexico before returning to the Kanawha Valley where he lived until 1927, still insisting he was an "unreconstructed and unregenerate rebel." W. Va. State Archives

Monument to Thornsberry Bailey Brown, first Union soldier to be killed in the war, May 22, 1861.

Gen. Henry Wise (1806-76), Confederate general and former governor of Virginia. He was in command of forces in the Kanawha Valley in July 1861 and under Gen. Lee in his western Virginia campaign until relieved of command in September 1861. HFNHP

BATTLE OF PHILIPPI

Col. George Porterfield, the Confederate commander, was sent to Grafton by Gen. Lee to recruit for the Confederate Army and to try to take control of the B and O Railroad. He met with little success, and threatened by strong Union forces from the west, he retreated to Philippi, Barbour County. There, on June 3rd, he was surprised by Federal troops under Col. Benjamin F. Kelley and routed. The Confederates retreated so fast that the battle is sometimes called the "Philippi Races." Although it was only a slight engagement, it was designated the first land battle of the Civil War, and it cleared the central part of West Virginia of rebel forces. No one was killed and only a few were wounded, including Col. Kelley, who was wounded in the chest, presumably by a Confederate escaping through an orchard. The colonel recovered, and his men presented him with a horse which he promptly named "Philippi."

Gen. Benjamin Franklin Kelley (1807-91), commander of Union forces at the Battle of Philippi. He was originally from Wheeling and spent most of the war in the state defending the Baltimore and Ohio Railroad. Author's Collection

Sketched by Mrs. M.D. Pool of Virginia.

TOWN of PHILLIPPI.

BARBOUR COUNTY, WEST VIRGINIA.

Place of the First Battle between the Federal and Confederate Armies.

1861.

The first land battle of the Civil War occurred at Philippi, Barbour County on June 3, 1861.

State of West Virginia

College Hill at Alderson-Broaddus College, Philippi. Site of the Union cannon that fired the first shot of the battle. This site has been altered considerably by the addition of a new building.

Union troops chasing the Confederates from Philippi.   State of West Virginia

The Philippi Bridge on Route 250 over the Tygart Valley River, built in 1852 by Lemuel Chenoweth. Both armies passed over it many times during the war, and it was used at one time as barracks for Union troops. It was thought to have been mined during the war in case Southern troops threatened it. The bridge was partially destroyed by fire in 1989 and reconstructed to its original appearance in 1991.

AN EARLY AMPUTATION

James E. Hanger, a Confederate cavalryman from Waynesboro, Va. was wounded by the first shell fired by Federal artillery at the Battle of Philippi. He was captured and had to have his leg amputated. During his convalescence, he designed and built, mainly from barrel staves, an artificial leg for himself and other wounded. After two months as a prisoner of war, he was exchanged at Norfolk, Va. Following his exchange, he was commissioned by the Confederate government to make artificial limbs for other soldiers, and he continued to do so after the war, founding a firm known as the J.E. Hanger Company. It is still in business today.

WALLACE'S RAID ON ROMNEY

Col. Lew Wallace of the Eleventh Indiana Infantry was stationed at Cumberland, Md., in June 1861. He had been notified of the presence of Confederate troops in Romney, Hampshire County.

On June 12 he set off with 500 men through New Creek and the rugged countryside in between to drive the enemy from the town. Close to town, on the 13th, his command was fired on by enemy pickets, and the town was warned of his coming.

The Confederates were subsequently driven from town, and the Union forces captured a few slaves and some supplies. Although this action was small and resulted in few casualties, it did alert Confederate Gen. Joseph Johnston's command farther east at Harpers Ferry that they, too, were vulnerable to attack, and they abandoned the town soon afterwards.

This occupation of Romney by Union troops was the first of at least 56 times that the town changed hands during the war. Only Winchester, Va. is reported to have surpassed Romney's record. There was no hard battle every time a change occurred. Sometimes the troops of one side would march out peaceably, and the other side's troops would enter and occupy the town.

Romney changed hands seven times in 1861, eight times in 1862, fourteen times in 1863, seventeen times in 1864 and ten times in 1865, the last time on April 15.

BATTLES OF RICH MOUNTAIN AND CORRICKS FORD

After the Philippi affair, Gen. McClellan took direct command at Clarksburg, Harrison County, while Gen. Lee appointed Gen. Robert S. Garnett to take over Southern forces. Garnett fortified positions at Laurel Hill near Belington, Barbour County, and Rich Mountain near Beverly. Both positions commanded the Parkersburg and Staunton Turnpike. After some characteristic long delays McClellan moved on the positions on July 10, 1861. He sent a force to Laurel Hill to make the Confederates think the main attack was to be there, and sent Gen. William S. Rosecrans on a long flanking movement to Rich Mountain, guided by David Hart, who lived on the mountaintop. The Confederates at Rich Mountain Ferry, under Lt. Col. John Pegram, were routed and retreated toward Beverly.

Gen. Garnett, stationed at Laurel Hill with 4,000 to 6,000 men, heard of the Rich Mountain disaster and decided to retreat toward Beverly. He saw troops at Beverly, and thinking they were Federals, backtracked to the north toward Parsons, Tucker County. The troops he saw were actually his own men retreating from Rich Mountain. The Rich Mountain defenders fell back to Laurel Hill but found it abandoned and 555 men surrendered to the Federals.

At Corricks Ford in Parsons, the Confederates fought a rear-guard action, and were again defeated, losing most of their wagon train. Gen. Garnett became the first general killed in the war. The Federals abandoned the pursuit, and the Southerners continued through Maryland to Hardy and Pendleton Counties and then to Monterey, Virginia.

The engagement at Rich Mountain was of great significance to the movement to form the new state. It influenced public opinion in the Trans-Allegheny section and helped establish the authority of the Restored Government, which made the formation of the state possible.

Gen. McClellan was called to Washington to take over a larger command on July 22, 1861.

Gen. William S. Rosecrans (1819-98), Commander of Union forces at the Battles of Rich Mountain and Carnifex Ferry. WVU Archives

The engagement at Belington, Barbour County, which occurred on July 8, 1861.   Author's Collection

Camp Laurel Hill site east of Belington. It is now the city water supply.

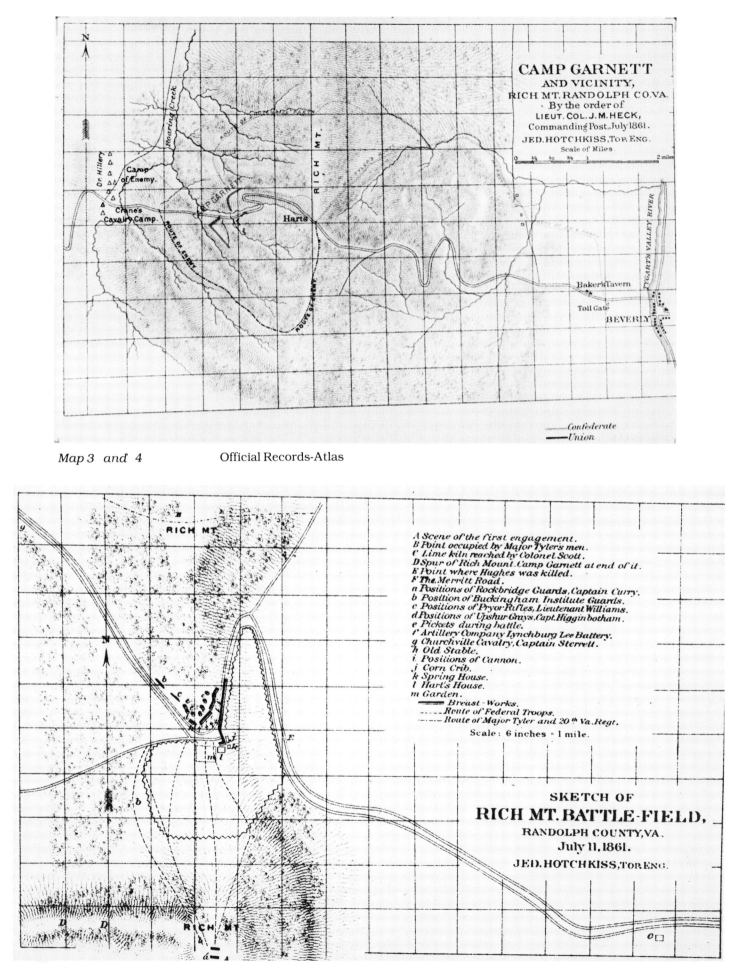

CAMP GARNETT
AND VICINITY,
RICH MT. RANDOLPH CO. VA.
By the order of
LIEUT. COL. J. M. HECK,
Commanding Post, July 1861.
JED. HOTCHKISS, TOP. ENG.
Scale of Miles

Confederate
Union

Map 3 and 4   Official Records-Atlas

A Scene of the first engagement.
B Point occupied by Major Tyler's men.
C Lime kiln reached by Colonel Scott.
D Spur of Rich Mount. Camp Garnett at end of it.
E Point where Hughes was killed.
F The Merritt Road.
a Positions of Rockbridge Guards, Captain Curry.
b Position of Buckingham Institute Guards.
c Positions of Pryor Rifles, Lieutenant Williams.
d Positions of Upshur Grays, Capt. Higginbotham.
e Pickets during battle.
f Artillery Company Lynchburg Lee Battery.
g Churchville Cavalry, Captain Sterrett.
h Old Stable.
i Positions of Cannon.
j Corn Crib.
k Spring House.
l Hart's House.
m Garden.
———— Breast-Works.
------- Route of Federal Troops.
—·—·— Route of Major Tyler and 20th Va. Regt.
Scale: 6 inches = 1 mile.

SKETCH OF
RICH MT. BATTLE-FIELD,
RANDOLPH COUNTY, VA.
July 11, 1861.
JED. HOTCHKISS, TOP. ENG.

Rich Mountain Battlefield site from the Union side looking north in July 1884. The Hart house and barn stood until 1940 when destroyed by fire. The house was used as a field hospital by Union forces.

Site of the Hart barn at the Rich Mountain battlefield.

Scene of the Rich Mountain battle. Soldiers' names which were carved on these rocks in 1861 can still be found.

The Battle of Rich Mountain, showing Indiana troops on the Beverly Pike and fighting around the Hart barn.

Author's Collection

Gen. Robert Garnett, commander of Confederate forces in western Virginia after their defeat at Philippi. He ordered a retreat from Laurel Hill after the Rich Mountain defeat and was killed at Corricks Ford, the first general killed in the Civil War, on July 13, 1861. He was a graduate of West Point and a commander of cadets there and participated in the Mexican War.   West Virginia Hillbilly

Discovery of the body of Gen. Garnett by Maj. Gordon and Col. Dumont of the Union Army after the battle. His body was returned to the Confederate troops for burial.   WVU Archives

Battle of Corricks Ford near Parsons, Tucker County on July 13, 1861.   WVU Archives

Looking upstream at Corricks Ford on Route 219.

PRYCE LEWIS – UNION SPY

There are many spy stories that came out of the Civil War. One of the earliest occurred in the Kanawha Valley.

Because the Union Army had no intelligence service at that time, Gen. George McClellan hired a civilian to gather information regarding enemy troop movements and disposition. The man he hired was Allan Pinkerton, a famous private detective.

Pinkerton sent a 29-year-old British subject, Pryce Lewis, one of his employees, who was to pose as the son of Lord Tray of England.

Lewis left Cincinnati with a servant on June 27, 1861 on the steamer *Cricket*. They landed at Guyandotte the next day, and Lewis decided to drop his disguise and get by as an ordinary English citizen.

The next morning, Lewis and his servant started towards the east, asking the way to White Sulphur Springs. Near the mouth of the Coal River they were picked up by Confederate pickets, taken to Camp Tompkins and brought before Capt. George S. Patton, second-in-command.

Lewis acted indignant about his detention, stating that he wanted to travel through the area to view the natural beauty before returning to England.

Patton was impressed by his guest and wrote him a pass to Charleston. Then the captain and the spy sat down to supper in the antebellum mansion at the camp. Patton boasted about his fortifications in the area and invited Lewis to inspect them, but Lewis declined in order not to appear too eager to see them.

At Charleston, the Union spy was introduced to Gen. Wise, who proved to be a very inhospitable host. He refused to issue a pass for a trip to Richmond, and Lewis and his servant were stranded in town for many days. Lewis tried pretending to write to the British Consul in Richmond, but that didn't work.

So the two agents put the delay to good use and picked up whatever information they could on Confederate forces in the area. When Gen. Wise left for a raid on Ripley on July 4, Lewis went to his friend, Col. C.Q. Tompkins, who informed him that a pass was not even needed to get to Richmond! Tompkins said that the road east was open to travel.

The two spies left Charleston immediately, but they did not head for Richmond. They wanted to report back to McClellan's headquarters as soon as possible and travelled south through Boone and Logan counties to Kentucky and then north to Cincinnati.

They had been away 19 days and travelled many miles through hundreds of enemy troops. When they returned, Lewis was sent back to Red House, Putnam County, to give his report on Confederate activity.

KANAWHA VALLEY CAMPAIGN

Meanwhile in the Kanawha Valley, Gen. Henry Wise, a former governor of Virginia, had occupied the valley west of Charleston, Kanawha County. The southern counties of western Virginia were more sympathetic to the Southern cause than the northern counties. An advertisement in the *Kanawha Valley Star* of May 28, 1861, printed in Charleston, read:

> *WANTED*
> *12,000 MEN*
>
> *The convention of Virginia have passed an ordinance for the organization of a Provisional Army of able-bodied men, capable and willing to defend their homes and rights are called upon to fill its ranks. It is provided that the same pay and allowances received by the army of the North shall be given to soldiers of the Provisional army. Monthly pay: Sergeants $17; Corporals $13; Privates $11; with liberal allowances of clothing and subsistence and medical attendence free of expense.*
>
> *1st Lt. L.W. Reid, Va. Forces*
> *Recruiting Officer*
> *Headquarters, Charleston, Kanawha County, Virginia*

An advertisement appeared in the *Richmond Enquirer* for recruits for the great adventure to come:

> *WISE'S LEGION*
>
> *We have been reliably informed that President Davis has authorized Gov. Wise to enlist a Brigade to act as a Partisan Legion, to be composed of cavalry and infantry. We predict for Wise's Legion a reputation equal to that of Lee's famous Legion of the Revolutionary War. Volunteers who wish early and active duty will do well to make prompt application to Gov. Wise at Richmond.*
>
> *Arms of all kinds; rifles, doublebarrel shotguns, sabres, and revolvers, private arms of every description, will be used by the Legion — Long range guns will not be needed, though not rejected by the Legion. Gov. Wise is not the man to stand at longrange.*
>
> *All cavalry companies who desire active duty should apply immediately. This must be the great arm of the Partisan Legion.*
>
> *Recruiting stations will be announced as soon as the primary organization has been completed.*
> *RICHMOND ENQUIRER*

BATTLE OF BARBOURSVILLE

Before the major clash of armies occurred in the Kanawha Valley at Scary Creek on July 17, 1861, there was a small skirmish at Barboursville, Cabell County, at that time the county seat. The action took place on July 14 at the Mud River bridge between five companies of the 2nd Kentucky (Union) and a larger combined force of Confederate troops from Camp Tompkins and local militia. The militia retreated in the face of a bayonet charge forcing the other troops to withdraw also. Only one Confederate was killed while the 2nd Kentucky lost five killed and 18 wounded.

The one Confederate wounded, Absolom Ballengee of Wayne County, was injured in the retreat. The right of way for the C and O Railroad was being prepared just before the war. A cut through a ridge was half-completed when the war broke out and left a drop of several feet. Ballengee, unmindful of this, ran over the precipice and sustained a broken leg. With his gun as a crutch, he painfully made his way back to his home.

SCARY CREEK

Scary Creek, on the west side of the Kanawha River opposite present day Nitro, was occupied by a force of Confederates under the command of Capt. George S. Patton, the grandfather of Gen. George S. Patton III of World War II fame.

On July 16, 1861 a detachment of the Federal Army under overall command of Gen. Jacob Cox of Ohio met a detachment of Southerners, who were on lookout duty, at the mouth of Poca River. A few shots were fired including several from Confederate cannon.

The next day, the main forces met at the mouth of Scary Creek, and at 9:00 a.m. the Confederate pickets were driven in from their position on Little Scary Creek. Then the Union cavalry broke into sight on an opposite ridge but withdrew in haste in face of fire from two cannon.

The battle itself was fought mainly at long range with rifle and artillery fire from each side of the creek. Several charges were made by the Federals on the bridge across Scary Creek, which the Confederates had fortified, but each was beaten back.

Capt. Patton was shot in the shoulder, and Capt. Albert Jenkins assumed command. As a third attack on the bridge was being readied, Confederate reinforcements arrived, and the Federals broke and ran. For some unexplained reason, Jenkins ordered his forces to withdraw. The probable explanation is that he saw the Federals falling back and probably thought that they were regrouping. At any rate, the battlefield was deserted by both sides. A Confederate colonel, however, recognized the situation, gathered a force together, returned to the field and claimed a Southern victory. The Federal loss was 14 killed, 30 wounded and 21 missing while the Confederates lost five killed and 26 wounded.

The Southern victory was short-lived, however. Upon learning of Gen. Garnett's defeat at Rich Mountain, Wise decided that his position was in danger because more Union troops were massing in the west and Rosecrans was moving down from Randolph County to Gauley Bridge. He departed the Kanawha Valley and reestablished his army in Greenbrier County. Thus by mid-July, Union forces controlled the vital area of the Kanawha Valley to Gauley Bridge.

A first sergeant in the 8th Virginia Cavalry sent to a Miss Sallie Young in Teays Valley, Putnam County the following poem he had written about Wise's retreat (from the Roy Bird Cook Collection at the WVU Archives):

WISE'S RETREAT FROM HAWKS NEST

Should old acquaintence be forgot
And never brought to mind
To think old Wise had run away
And left one hog behind

He stole away the last old goose
He eat the ------* cow
He did not spare the -----* horse
But left one poor old sow.

He used up all the oats and corn
He fed up all the hay
And when the eleventh came in sight
Old Wise he ran away

He ran so fast he could not stop
For valley and for hill
He had no time to call around
To pay his washing bill

And when old Gabriel blow his horn
And the devil claim his own
May he throw wide his arms
To welcome old Wise home

And when he takes old Wise below
With Jenkins and his host
May he, with fear and trembling
No longer swear and boast

When Floyd comes home to meet him
Which he is sure to do
May the devil and his angels
Put both the traitors through

But, good devil, be you careful
And give them all they need
Or, by the great old Moses
They'll get mad and secede

Watch Floyd in every movement
Be sure to guard him well
For if you don't be careful
He'll steal Wise out of h-ll.

* Illegible

Site of the Battle of Barboursville, Cabell County. The Confederates were on top of the hill, the Federals stationed in the foreground. A bridge crossed the Mud River here. Gary Bays

Gen. Jacob Cox (1828-1900), commander of the "Brigade of the Kanawha" at the beginning of the war and Union commander at the Battle of Scary Creek on July 17, 1861. He was head of the Department of the Kanawha until August 1862, Governor of Ohio, 1867-69 and Secretary of the Interior, 1869-70. USAMHI

Capt. George S. Patton, commander of Confederate forces at Scary Creek. Patton fought in many of the battles in West Virginia and rose to the rank of Colonel. He was killed at the Third Battle of Winchester in 1864. Author's collection

Pryce Lewis, Union spy, on the left toasts Capt. George Patton at his headquarters at Camp Tompkins near present-day St. Albans, Kanawha County.
Terry Lowry

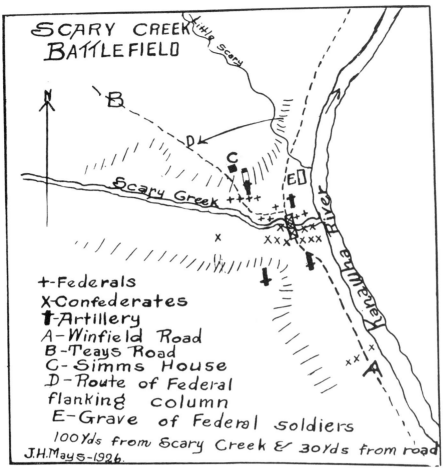

SCARY CREEK
BATTLEFIELD

+ -Federals
X-Confederates
† -Artillery
A -Winfield Road
B -Teays Road
C -Simms House
D -Route of Federal
flanking column
E -Grave of Federal soldiers
100 Yds from Scary Creek & 30Yds from road
J.H.Mays-1926.

Map 5

Drawn by Pvt. James H. Mays, of Co. F, 22nd Va. Inf. (Rocky Point
Greys from Monroe County), who arrived on the scene at the conclusion
of the battle.   Terry Lowry.

*Intersection of the Teays Valley and Winfield roads in Putnam County, scene of the Scary Creek battle.
Simms Hill is in the background.*
                                                           Terry Lowry

Morgan's Kitchen Museum at St. Albans, Kanawha County on Route 60. It was built in 1846 and was originally at Morgan's farm near Scary Creek. Union troops were fed from here the day before the battle at Scary Creek.

Littlepage House on Kanawha Two-Mile on Charleston's West Side. It overlooked the Confederate Camp, Two-Mile, established by Gen. Wise in June 1861, commanding the junction of Ripley road and the Valley road into Charleston. Terry Lowry

GENERAL LEE'S CAMPAIGN

After Garnett's death Gen. Lee came to West Virginia on August 3, 1861, on a tour of inspection and consultation on the plan of campaign. His immediate purpose was to drive the Union force, commanded by Gen. John J. Reynolds, from positions at Elkwater, Randolph County, which controlled the Huttonsville-Huntersville Pike, and from the Cheat Mountain Summit Fort on the Parkersburg and Staunton Pike. Lee had approximately 15,000 men in the area but had great difficulty because of the almost daily rainfall in August and September. Measles also took a heavy toll. Lee's campaign in this area failed in part because of the failure of his subordinate officers to give him their wholehearted support.

Lee ordered Gen. W.W. Loring to move up the road toward Huttonsville and attack the Cheat Mountain fort, but Loring waited until he could get supplies. Lee then went to Valley Mountain near Mace, Pocahontas County, on the Huttonsville Pike, to scout the area and found that the Union troops were fortifying the road. It had rained for 20 days and the road was almost impassable. On Aug. 12 Loring moved to Valley Mountain and Lee formed his plan to attack from three directions. The plan went well for a while but did not succeed partly because of a lack of coordination. The main forces that were to attack the Cheat Mountain fort thought there were 4,000 troops at the fort, when actually there were only 300, so they did not attack.

On Sept. 13, while on scouting duty at Elkwater, Lt. Col. John A. Washington, the last owner of Mount Vernon and an aide-de-camp to Gen. Lee, was killed by Union troops. This greatly disturbed Lee, who was a close friend of Col. Washington.

An early portrait of Gen. Robert E. Lee (1807-70), commander of forces in western Virginia in the fall of 1861.   W. Va. State Archives

Monument erected in memory of Lt. Col. John A. Washington, south of Elkwater, Randolph County on Route 219. He was an Aide-de-Camp to General Lee and the last owner of Mount Vernon. Killed here on Sept. 13, 1861. The monument was placed here in 1926 by the Randolph Chapter, Daughters of the Confederacy.

Drawing of Cheat Mountain near Cheat Bridge in Randolph County just off Route 219. The camp was built in 1861 and occupied by Union forces during the war. Its elevation was the highest of any encampment occupied by Union troops during the war. Drawn by a soldier of the 2nd West Virginia Infantry.

WVU Archives

Cheat Mountain fort looking east. Arrows point to outer limits of the fort.

Breastwork remains at the Cheat Mountain fort.

BATTLE OF CROSS LANES

The Battle of Cross Lanes near Carnifex Ferry in Nicholas County, was fought on August 26, 1861, between the Federals under Col. E.B. Tyler, commanding the 7th Regiment of Ohio Volunteer Infantry, and Brig. Gen. John B. Floyd, commanding the Confederates, whose forces are thought to have consisted of at least three regiments of infantry, a company of cavalry and three pieces of artillery. The Confederates attacked at about 5 a.m. while the Federals were preparing breakfast. The battle lasted about one hour, and the forces of Col. Tyler were completely routed. The Federal loss was 15 killed, 20 wounded and 38 taken prisoner. The Confederate loss was 5 killed and 6 wounded.

Col. Tyler and about 200 men escaped to Gauley Bridge, another 400 men returned through the mountains to Elk River and thence to Charleston and Gauley Bridge. Several other stragglers retreated through the forest to Gauley Bridge.

The dead were buried and the wounded cared for by Gen. Floyd's troops, and in his report to Gen. Robert E. Lee, Floyd said: "Tyler's command is said to be of their best troops. They were certainly brave men."

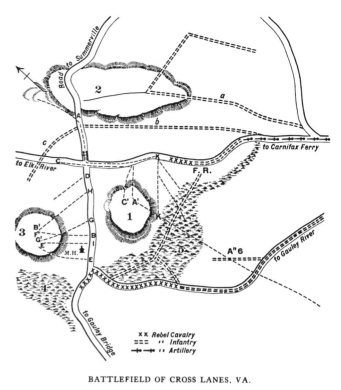

BATTLEFIELD OF CROSS LANES, VA.

August 26th, 1861

Map 6

Part of the camp of Col. Erastus B. Tyler at Kesslers Cross Lanes in August 1861.   Library of Congress

-41-

Gen. Rosecrans' headquarters at Kesslers Cross Lanes.

Site of the Battle of Cross Lanes on Route 129 in Nicholas County. The battle was fought on Aug. 26, 1861 as a prelude to the Carnifex Ferry engagement.

CARNIFEX FERRY
SEWELL MOUNTAIN

General William S. Rosecrans had taken over as Union Commander in West Virginia upon McClellan's recall to Washington. Gen. Jacob Cox held a fortified post at Gauley Bridge and patrolled the area. The Confederates, following Lee's plan, hoped to regain the Kanawha Valley, but the continuing quarrel between Gen. Wise and Gen. John Floyd, both ex-governors of Virginia and political antagonists, kept the army from being united. Floyd was overall commander in the area because of his earlier commission date, but Wise kept burdening Lee with criticisms of Floyd.

After the Confederate victory at Cross Lanes, Gen. Floyd established his command on the bluffs overlooking Carnifex Ferry and named it "Camp Gauley." The ferry was at a strategic crossing of the Gauley River, one of the few places where a large force could cross the river.

With the Confederates now controlling communications between the Kanawha Valley and Clarksburg, Gen. Rosecrans was determined to drive the enemy from the area and he advanced on "Camp Gauley."

To protect his position, Floyd had extensive entrenchments constructed, extending across a rugged, jutting strip of land formed by a bend in the Gauley River. He considered these fortifications a formidable obstacle to any Union advance.

Floyd had about 2,000 troops at "Camp Gauley" and a total of 6,200 scattered in the area. An additional 1,600 men were on the way from the east to reinforce him.

Wise was ordered to bring his troops up from the Gauley Bridge area where he was putting pressure on the Union troops there. Due to transportation problems and his own obstinancy, only part of his command arrived in time for the battle.

The Union forces advanced south from Clarksburg on August 31 to relieve pressure on the Kanawha Valley and attack the Confederate force. Over 6,000 troops marched down the Gauley Bridge-Weston Turnpike toward "Camp Gauley," and attacked the enemy position on September 10.

The battle lasted all day with the superior Union force failing to dislodge the Confederates. That night, Floyd decided to abandon the fight and "Camp Gauley" to the larger enemy force. His command made an orderly retreat down the road to the ferry and escaped south to Meadow Bluff in Greenbrier County where Gen. Lee was waiting for them.

Gen. Wise was ordered to retreat from the west and marched along the James River and Kanawha Turnpike to the summit of Big Sewell Mountain which he proceeded to fortify.

The battle resulted in 158 Union and 20 Confederate casualties. It was important in that it kept control of the Kanawha Valley and much of western Virginia firmly in Union hands.

On Sept. 22 Lee arrived at Sewell Mountain but could not get much information on the enemy because of the lack of cavalry and the constant battle between the two Confederate commanders. Wise was finally ordered back to Richmond and by Sept. 29 most of the Confederate force had been consolidated with Lee's troops at Sewell. Meanwhile, the Union forces had taken up positions facing Lee and for two weeks the forces opposed each other with no decisive results. With no results forthcoming Rosecrans withdrew from his positions on Oct. 5. A threatened attack west of Staunton and the cold weather kept Lee from taking advantage of the withdrawal. On Oct. 20 Lee gave up further offensive movements and ordered troops to withdraw toward Lewisburg, Greenbrier County. Lee was recalled to Virginia and thus the Trans-Allegheny Virginia area was not secured for the South.

Gen. Lee had been shown a horse at his camp at the summit of Big Sewell Mountain. It was born and raised near Blue Sulphur Springs and was four years old in 1861. Lee purchased the horse from Maj. Thomas Broun later in the year and it was delivered to him in December at his new post in South Carolina. It cost him $200 and he named it "Traveller." The horse was to carry him throughout the war and outlived him by many years.

Gen. John Floyd (1806-63), Confederate general, former governor of Virginia and President Buchanan's Secretary of War. He was commander of forces under Gen. Lee in his 1861 western Virginia campaign and commander at the Battle of Carnifex Ferry on Sept. 10, 1861.

W. Va. State Archives

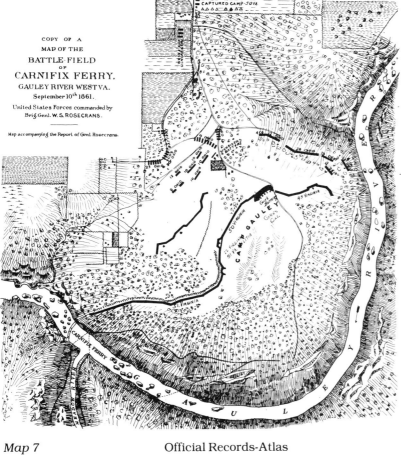

COPY OF A
MAP OF THE
BATTLE-FIELD
OF
CARNIFIX FERRY,
GAULEY RIVER WEST VA.
September 10th 1861.

United States Forces commanded by
Brig. Genl. W. S. ROSECRANS.

Map accompanying the Report of Genl. Rosecrans.

Map 7   Official Records-Atlas

*A foxhole on the Patteson Trail at the Carnifex
Ferry Battlefield State Park. Part of the battle
took place in these woods.*

Entered according to act of Congress in the year 1862 by J Nep Roesler in the Clerks office of the District Court of the Southern District of Ohio

ard Comp G 47 th Reg t OV-USA

Printed by Ehrgott, Forbriger & C? Cincinnati

BATTLE AT CARNIFAX FERRY.

Roesler's print vividly portrays the Carnifex Ferry Battle on Sept. 10, 1861.

W. Va. State Archives

An authentic reproduction of a 6-pound cast iron James gun used by the Federals at Carnifex Ferry.

The Patteson House at Carnifex Ferry Battlefield State Park just off Route 129 in Nicholas County. The house was used as a Federal hospital and has been completely restored by the state.

Carnifex Ferry on the Gauley River as it looks today.

Floyd's command recrossing the Gauley River after the battle on Sept. 10. The Meadow River empties into the Gauley at this point.
W.Va. Dept. of Natural Resources

View from the top of Sewell Mountain in Fayette County on Route 60. Busters Knob is in the background. Both armies fortified these hills for several months in the fall of 1861.

Site of the Lee Tree atop Sewell Mountain, Fayette County on Route 60. The original tree, which stood until 1937, marked the spot where Gen. Robert E. Lee camped in September 1861 and was shown a horse which he eventually bought and used throughout the war. This was the horse he named "Traveller." The original tree was cut down in 1936.

NICHOLAS COUNTY

Nicholas County was a border county during the war and sentiments were strong on both sides. Many people had to flee their homes because of their alliance to one side or the other. Rebecca Harding Davis, a resident of the county, wrote of conditions there: "I write from the border of the battlefield, and I find no theme for shallow argument or flimsy rhymes. The shadow of death has fallen on us; it chills the very heaven. No child laughs in my face as I pass the home. Men here have forgotten to hope, forgotten to pray; only in the bitterness of endurance they say in the morning, 'Would God it were evening!' and in the evening 'Would God it were morning!'"

BATTLE OF GREENBRIER RIVER

After the campaign at Cheat Mountain the Confederates withdrew to the present town of Bartow, Pocahontas County, at the crossing of the Greenbrier River and the Parkersburg and Staunton Turnpike. The hills surrounding this junction were fortified and named Camp Bartow.

On Oct. 3, Gen. John J. Reynolds, in command of Union forces in the Cheat Mountain area, sent his troops to dislodge the enemy and open up the turnpike. Although he had a superior force, the Confederates had a better position, and upon seeing reinforcements coming down the turnpike from Camp Allegheny, Reynolds broke off the engagement and returned to Cheat Mountain.

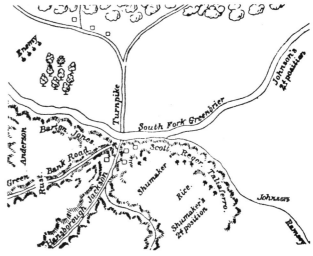

CAMP BARTOW, GREENBRIER RIVER,
October 3, 1861.

Map 8   Pocahontas County Historical Society

Mountainous terrain between Gauley Bridge and Sewell Mountain as portrayed in this drawing from Harper's Weekly, *Oct. 5, 1861. This terrain precluded the easy movement of troops by both sides.*   Author's Collection

BARBOURSVILLE
Nov. 1861 . 34th Reg! O. V. I.

The 34th Regiment of Ohio Volunteer Infantry at Barboursville, Cabell County in November 1861.   Barboursville Chapter DAR

Camp Bartow, in Bartow, Pocahontas County, was constructed by the Confederates in early 1861 to guard the Parkersburg and Staunton Turnpike. This was the scene of a battle on Oct. 3, 1861 in which the defenders turned back a superior force of Union troops.

Charleston's West Side where the first military execution in West Virginia and one of the first of the war took place on Dec. 20, 1861. Pvt. Richard Gatewood, of Co. C, 1st Kentucky Infantry, who was stationed at Gauley Bridge under Gen. Jacob Cox, was court-martialed for desertion, threatening an officer and assaulting a fellow soldier. Gen. Cox personally took charge of the execution in the interest of keeping discipline among his troops.   Author's Collection

TOP OF ALLEGHENY BATTLE

An outstanding example of a Civil War campground and battlefield is well preserved at Top of Allegheny just off Route 250 in Pocahontas County. More than 4,200 feet of trenches, gun emplacements and cabin sites are visible. The site straddles the Parkersburg and Staunton Turnpike and was a campground for Confederate troops in the winter of 1861-62. In elevation (4,250 feet) it was the highest Confederate winter campground of the war. Union Gen. Robert Milroy marched through Camp Bartow and on Dec. 13 attacked the entrenched Confederates and was repulsed with a loss of 137 killed and wounded. He retreated to Randolph County. The Confederates held the area through April 1862 and then abandoned the region for the rest of the war because of bad weather at the site.

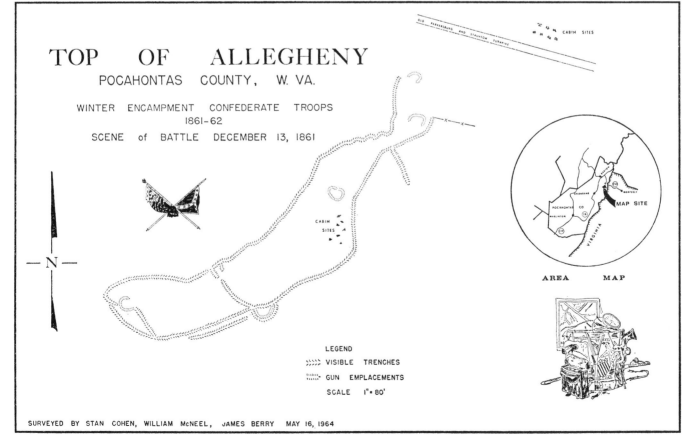

Map 9   -51-

Top of Allegheny fort and campground site, Pocahontas County, just off Route 250 near the Virginia border. Scene of a battle on Dec. 13, 1861. Trenches, gun emplacements and chimney piles left from huts built by the Confederate soldiers in the winter of 1861-62 are still plainly visible.

OTHER ENGAGEMENTS 1861

Many other engagements took place during the year. Col. John C. Starkweather defeated Stonewall Jackson at Falling Waters, Berkeley County, on July 2. This was Jackson's first skirmish of the war. A clash at Belington, Barbour County, on July 8 resulted in a defeat for Gen. Morris and the left wing of McClellan's army, who attempted to drive the Confederates from the woods at the rear of the village. Gen. Wise with 1,250 men attacked an equal number of Federals at Hawks Nest, Fayette County, on September 2 but was repulsed.

At Guyandotte, Cabell County, on Nov. 10, 150 Union recruits were surprised and cut to pieces by Confederate raiders. Among the Union prisoners taken was Uriah Payne, of Ohio, who had been the first soldier to plant the U.S. Flag at Monterey, Mexico, during the Mexican War. Then Union troops crossed to Guyandotte from Ohio, and the Southerners retreated. A portion of Guyandotte was burned by the Federals.

Sutton, Braxton County, was captured by 135 Confederates on Dec. 29, and they burned part of the town. The next day an expedition of 400 Union troops marched into Webster County in pursuit of the soldiers who had torched Sutton. They were overtaken at Glades, and in the ensuing fight 22 Confederates were killed and 29 houses believed to belong to Rebel bushwackers were burned.

The year ended with most of western Virginia controlled by the Union. Gen. Rosecrans commanded the region with 40,000 troops. Cox was in the Kanawha Valley, Milroy in the Cheat Mountain area, and Kelley guarded the B and O Railroad. The Confederate Army was not large enough to retake the area.

Gen. Robert Milroy, commander of Union troops at the Top of Allegheny Battle on Dec. 13. He participated in many campaigns in the state during the war. WVU Archives

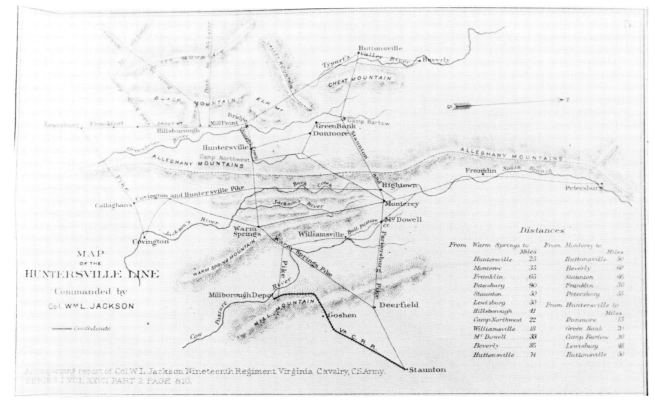

Map 10

HARPERS FERRY

One of the most historic sites in the United States lies at the eastern tip of West Virginia at the junction of the Potomac and Shenandoah rivers in Jefferson County.

Robert Harper purchased the site in 1747 from a Peter Stephens and established a ferry and mill, and the little town that grew up around them was named Harpers Ferry.

George Washington selected this as the site of a national armory because of abundant water power, a supply of iron and extensive hardwood forests which provided a source of charcoal. Arms made here could be floated down the Potomac to Washington, D.C. In 1819, Hall's Rifle Works was established and thus began the first mass production of breechloading rifles with interchangeable parts.

Because the town was in a natural gap through the Blue Ridge Mountains, the Chesapeake and Ohio Canal reached it in 1833 and ultimately was extended to Cumberland, Maryland. The Baltimore and Ohio Railroad reached the town in 1834 and eventually was expanded to the Ohio River. Both methods of transportation played an important part in the coming Civil War.

If the town was unknown in the 1850s, it gained national attention in 1859 with John Brown's raid on the Federal Arsenal.

The Civil War brought disaster to Harpers Ferry. When Confederate forces, eager to obtain the machinery for manufacturing arms, which they were short of, advanced on the town on April 18, 1861, the Federal officer in charge of the post destroyed the arsenal and 4,300 rifles and muskets. Some of the salvaged equipment, however, was shipped south for use in the Confederacy's arms production after the town was occupied.

Early in 1861, Col. T.J. (later "Stonewall") Jackson commanded troops on Bolivar Heights. During this time he managed to concentrate railroad equipment from the area and to send it to Martinsburg. The town was determined to be untenable, however, and the Confederates abandoned it on June 15 after burning the railroad bridges and supplies that could not be carried off.

When Union troops removed a large amount of wheat from the mill on Virginius Island during the fall of 1861, Confederate cavalry troops raided the town and burned the mill. A few months later a Union scout was killed by a sniper's bullet fired from a building in the lower part of the town. In retaliation, Union troops burned most of the lower town.

Harpers Ferry changed hands several times during the war, the most dramatic time occuring during Lee's Maryland campaign in September 1862. Following Lee's victory at Second Manassas, he invaded Maryland. As he reached Frederick, intending to proceed through Hagerstown into Pennsylvania, he realized that the garrison at Harpers Ferry posed a threat to his line of supplies.

Lee divided his army into four units, and one unit approached Harpers Ferry from three directions to try to take the town and the Union garrison stationed there. Gen. Jackson's command marched from Frederick to Martinsburg and came up from the south to cut off any means of escape from that direction. Gen. McLaw's command crossed South Mountain and occupied Maryland Heights opposite the town. Gen. Walker's command was to destroy an aqueduct on the C and O Canal across the Monocacy River then occupy Loudoun Heights opposite the town.

The execution of this complicated plan was made more difficult for Gen. Lee when one of his couriers lost a copy of the orders, and they were found by the enemy. Gen. McClellan now became aware of the weak position of his foe.

Col. Dixon Miles, in command of the Harpers Ferry garrison, had great difficulty in communicating with McClellan. The latter hoped the garrison could hold out until he could rescue them, but by September 12 McLaw's and Jackson's troops were in position. Walker was delayed by an unsuccessful attempt to destroy the aqueduct but occupied Loudoun Heights on the 13th.

Union troops on Bolivar Heights and Camp Hill were in a difficult position, bombarded by Confederate guns on the surrounding hills. The Union cavalry escaped across a pontoon bridge over the Potomac but after two days of intense fire, Gen. Miles surrendered about 12,500 troops. He had suffered 44 killed and 173 wounded. Gen. Miles was subsequently killed by a cannon shot after the flag of truce was raised. It was a great victory for the Confederate forces.

Gen. Jackson assigned Gen. A.P. Hill to parole the Union prisoners and he hurried north to join Lee's main army at Sharpsburg, Maryland. Hill's troops soon followed.

Thus, the last large battle in the vicinity of Harpers Ferry came to an end. The town and arsenal lay in ruins and would never again regain their former economic status.

It was not until 1944 that Congress authorized the establishment of a national monument at the town site, preserving this historic spot for all Americans.

Harpers Ferry, Jefferson County as it looked in 1860.

HFNHP

Harpers Ferry, Jefferson County, now part of the Harpers Ferry National Historical Park, National Park Service.

State of West Virginia

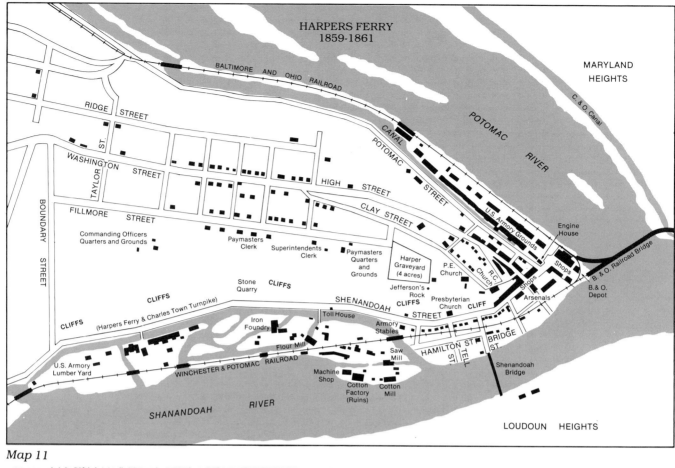

HARPERS FERRY
1859-1861

MARYLAND
HEIGHTS

BALTIMORE AND OHIO RAILROAD

C. & O. Canal

RIDGE STREET

POTOMAC RIVER

CANAL

POTOMAC STREET

WASHINGTON STREET

TAYLOR ST.

HIGH STREET

U.S. Armory Grounds

Engine House

FILLMORE STREET

CLAY STREET

BOUNDARY STREET

Commanding Officers
Quarters and Grounds

Paymasters
Clerk

Superintendents
Clerk

Paymasters
Quarters
and
Grounds

Harper
Graveyard
(4 acres)

P.E.
Church

R.C.
Church

Shops

B. & O. Railroad Bridge

Stone
Quarry

CLIFFS

Jefferson's
Rock

Presbyterian
Church

Arsenals

B. & O.
Depot

CLIFFS

SHENANDOAH STREET

CLIFFS

CLIFF

(Harpers Ferry & Charles Town Turnpike)

Iron
Foundry

Toll House

Armory
Stables

HAMILTON ST.

BRIDGE ST.

CLIFFS

Flour Mill

TELL ST.

Shenandoah
Bridge

U.S. Armory
Lumber Yard

WINCHESTER & POTOMAC RAILROAD

Saw
Mill

Machine
Shop

Cotton
Factory
(Ruins)

Cotton
Mill

SHANANDOAH RIVER

LOUDOUN HEIGHTS

Map 11

Evacuation and burning of the U.S. Arsenal at Harpers Ferry on the night of April 18, 1861 by Federal troops to keep it from falling into the hands of the advancing Confederates.   HFNHP

-56-

The entrance to the U.S. Armory grounds with the fire enginehouse on the left. The machine shops where the muskets were assembled are on the right. This view was taken before 1861. HFNHP

The remains of the U.S. Armory in 1862. Harpers Ferry would not regain its prominent pre-war role after 1865. USAMHI

Harpers Ferry in July 1861, showing damage after Confederates had withdrawn from the town.   HFNHP

The destroyed bridge pier is still intact across the Potomac River. The railroad tunnel is located at Maryland Heights.

High Street (old Highway 340) leading up the hill to Bolivar Heights. Many souvenir shops are located along this street.

Restored buildings in Harpers Ferry National Historical Park.

Trenches are still visible at the KOA Campground to the east of Harpers Ferry.

Gen. Jackson's headquarters in June 1861.

Map 12

BOLIVAR HEIGHTS

Bolivar Heights was a natural barrier along a ridge just east of Harpers Ferry and proved to be a formidable obstruction to any western force trying to take Harpers Ferry. There is a long line of Union troop entrenchments still intact, and at the south end is an artillery fortification named Battery One. It was constructed in September 1862 as part of the town's defenses and was designed to hold from four to six field pieces.

The Battle of Bolivar Heights was fought on Oct. 16, 1861, when 500 Confederates, under Lt. Col. Turner Ashby were pitted against a slightly superior Union force commanded by Col. John Geary. The Confederates withdrew after several hours of intermittent skirmishing.

A serious attempt at fortifying the ridge did not take place until mid-September 1862 when trenches were hastily constructed to block Gen. Stonewall Jackson's attempt to encircle and capture the Union garrison. Jackson, however, did succeed and the 12,500 Union troops surrendered on the heights.

After the battle of Antietam in September 1862, over 60,000 Union troops under Gen. George McClellan were inspected on the heights by President Lincoln.

Union cannon and trenches at Bolivar Heights.

GAULEY BRIDGE

Situated at the junction of the New and Gauley Rivers and astride the James River and Kanawha Turnpike, Gauley Bridge was a very important supply depot for Union forces. One road north led to Cross Lanes, Carnifex Ferry, Summersville, Weston and Sutton and the town was the crossroads for all communications in the northwest part of the state. All important movements from the east into southwest Virginia had to go through here and it formed an important link in the chain of posts designed to cover the Ohio Valley from invasion. It was the most advanced outpost to protect the Kanawha Valley and thus was highly prized by both sides early in the war. Since the country to the east was very difficult and rugged, no sustained military operations could take place there.

The town had to be supplied from the Virginia and Tennessee Railroad at Narrows, Va. on the New River over the mountains from the east or north or from the Kanawha Valley in the west. Along with outposts at Huttonsville, Cheat Mountain and Elkwater it guarded this part of the state below the B and O Railroad.

At the start of the war, the town was in Confederate territory. Brig. Gen. Henry Wise was raising troops in the Kanawha Valley along with Col. John McCausland and Col. C.Q. Tompkins. They had troops stationed in Gauley Bridge and throughout the rest of the valley.

Col. Christopher Q. Tompkins, a prominent farmer and retired army officer had moved to the area before the war and built one of the finest homes in the vicinity, above the town and at the present site of the Hawks Nest Golf Course. It was called "Gauley Mount" and burned down during the war. When the war began, Tompkins, a West Point graduate, joined the Confederate Army.

After the battle of Scary Creek in Putnam County on July 17, 1861, Wise retreated to Gauley Bridge and then into Greenbrier County. The saga of the two bridges across the Gauley River begins here.

A sturdy covered bridge had been constructed in 1850 to replace the former dilapidated one. It was a major link on the James River and Kanawha Turnpike. As Wise retreated east, it was an easy task to set the wooden bridge on fire to slow the pursuing Federal forces. The Miller store, which still stands in town, was barely saved. The intense fire lit up the darkened sky for miles.

Tompkin's farm was taken over by Union forces and renamed Camp Tompkins. Maj. Rutherford B. Hayes, a future president of the United States, but then, judge-advocate general on Gen. Rosecrans' staff, was stationed at the camp in the fall of 1861.

During the fall and winter of 1861-62, the area was a major supply depot for Union forces under the overall command of Gen. Jacob Cox.

The covered bridge over Gauley River. This bridge was constructed in 1850 and burned by Confederate troops on July 27, 1861. A new bridge was constructed on these piers and destroyed, probably by Union troops, in September 1862.
Fayette County Historical Society

The second bridge at Gauley Bridge was built in February 1862 and supposedly burned by Union troops in September 1862 on their retreat from Gen. Loring's troops. It was not until 1926 that a new bridge was built across the river.   WVU Archives

The old bridge piers still standing in the Gauley River supported at least two bridges destroyed during the war.

In January 1862, new bridge construction was commenced on the old piers by a firm from Philadelphia. In 23 days, a 585-foot suspension bridge was finished. It was a remarkable job under wartime conditions.

This bridge, however, did not last long. It became a victim of Gen. Joseph A. Lightburn's retreat from the Kanawha Valley in September 1862, with the advance of Gen. William Loring's troops. There has always been conjecture as to who destroyed the second bridge. It is most probable that the Union forces, with some difficulty, burned the bridge on Sept. 11, 1862.

That day was one of confusion for Federal forces. The Confederates had posted an artillery piece on Cotton Hill and were shelling both Gauley Bridge and Glen Ferris. The Federal wagon train and rear guard troops had difficulty in their retreat down the turnpike because of the constant enemy fire.

The cannon that had fired from Cotton Hill was supposedly pushed over the hill into a ravine as the Confederates were in such a hurry to get to the abandoned supplies in Gauley Bridge. In August 1953, the *Charleston Daily Mail* sponsored a major search for the cannon. The site from which the cannon was fired and a cannon ball were found, but the cannon was never found. It probably was hauled off for scrap years before, if in fact it was ever thrown into the ravine in the first place.

In the Federal's haste to evacuate the area, they apparently blew up their large ammo dump at Zoll's Hollow opposite Glen Ferris. Debris from this dump can still be found today.

Camp Maskell (later Camp Reynolds) was established in the fall of 1862 at the present site of Kanawha Falls on the south side of the Kanawha River, two miles below Gauley Bridge. The constant threat of Confederate forces in the area mandated the stationing of troops there in the winter of 1862-63.

Hayes was posted to Camp Reynolds for the winter along with 2nd Lt. William McKinley, also a future president.

After this winter, the war bypassed the area and it remained in Federal hands for the remaining two years.

Zoll's Hollow, opposite Glen Ferris, site of the Federal ammo dump that was blown up in September 1862. Shell fragments and bullets can still be found here.

Col. Christopher Q. Tompkins, prominent Gauley Bridge resident, graduate of West Point and Confederate officer. Virginia State Archives

Camp Tompkins as it looked during the war.   WVU Archives

The site of Camp Tompkins on Hawks Nest Mountain which is now occupied by the Hawks Nest Golf Course. The property was owned by Col. Christopher Q. Tompkins, a very prominent area farmer and retired army officer.

CAMP, GAULEY BRIDGE.

Roesler's print shows the hand-operated Union ferry beside the abandoned bridge piers. The present-day Miller's tavern is shown at the far end of the piers.
WVU Archives

A Union battery on Hawks Nest Mountain looking east as drawn by Roesler.
W. Va. State Archives

VIEW FROM HAWK'S NEST

Gun emplacement near the Hawks Nest Country Club on Route 60. This was part of Camp Tompkins.

Miller's Tavern on Route 39 in Gauley Bridge. The collector of tolls for the covered bridge across Gauley River once lived here. Before the war it was a stage stop. General Cox used the building as his headquarters in 1861 and General Lightburn in 1862. It is now an apartment complex.

Camp Reynolds at Kanawha Falls. Sketched by J.W. Oswald of the Union Army.

Winter headquarters (1862-63) of the 23rd Ohio Volunteer Infantry at Camp Reynolds at Kanawha Falls, Fayette County. It was first called Camp Maskell but later renamed Camp Reynolds in honor of Maj. Eugene E. Reynolds. He was killed at the Battle of South Mountain, Md. This view of the log huts was taken on Jan. 4, 1863.

Two rifle pits located at the Camp Reynolds camp site. The Kanawha River is in the background.
Gary Bays

A carving on Van Bibber rock at Camp Reynolds can still be seen today. Jno. Day, Jr. was a member of the 23rd Ohio Volunteer Infantry stationed at the camp. Gary Bays

Trenches can still be traced at the Camp Reynolds site. Gary Bays

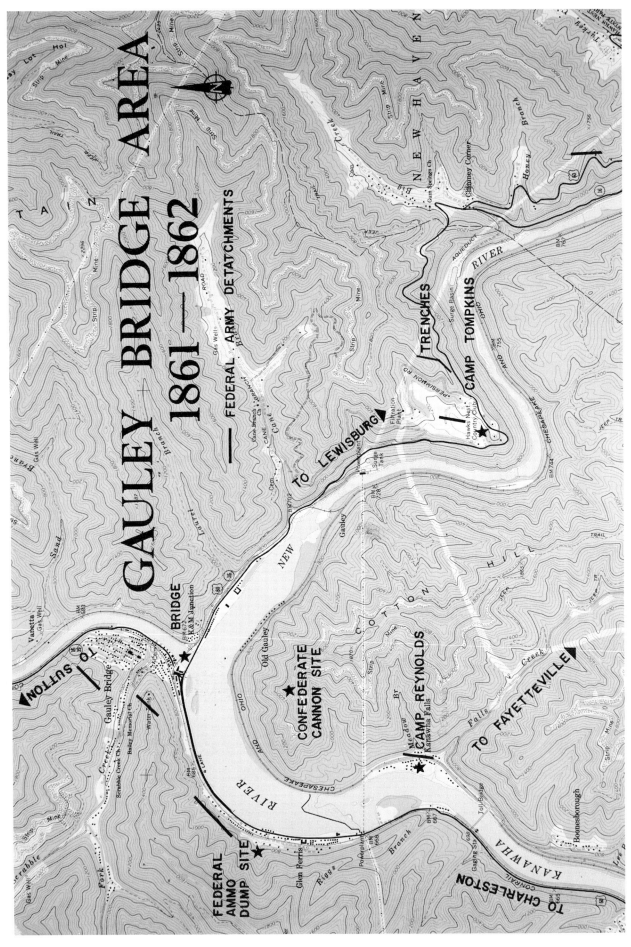

GAULEY BRIDGE AREA
1861—1862

—— FEDERAL ARMY DETACHMENTS

TO LEWISBURG

TRENCHES

CAMP TOMPKINS

BRIDGE
K&M Junction

TO SUTTON

Gauley Bridge

CONFEDERATE
CANNON SITE

CAMP REYNOLDS
Kanawha Falls

TO FAYETTEVILLE

FEDERAL
AMMO
DUMP SITE

TO CHARLESTON

NEW RIVER

KANAWHA

Map 13

CROSSING LOUP CREEK OR RIVER

Roesler's prints of action in Fayette and Nicholas counties in 1861.

CROSSING TO FAYETTEVILLE

BEVERLY

Like Gauley Bridge, Beverly was to become a very strategic spot to both armies during the war. The small town in Randolph County straddled the important Parkersburg and Staunton Turnpike and the Beverly and Fairmont Turnpike. It was on the eastern flank of Rich Mountain, an important pass through the Allegheny chain. Whoever controlled the town had a good base of operations for striking north to the B and O Railroad or south into the Cheat Mountain area which opened up a possible invasion into the Greenbrier Valley or a blocking of the Kanawha Valley.

In the opening days of the war, the town was turned into a major Confederate supply depot, but after their defeat at Rich Mountain, the Confederates withdrew and the Federals reoccupied the town.

Immediately after the Rich Mountain battle, the first news of McClellan's victory was sent out to the nation by telegraph. The message was sent from the first telegraph office to be set up permanently during a war, on the second floor of the Adam Crawford home. The house is still standing on U.S. 219 in the town center.

A love story evolved when Harriet Crawford, a resident of the house, fell in love with one of the Union telegraphers. She said she could not marry a Union man, however, so he deserted his unit, escaped over Rich Mountain to Huttonsville, and joined the Confederate Army. The couple was later married and lived in Beverly.

After McClellan's troops occupied the town in June 1861, they located on the three high ridges known as Mt. Iser, which overlooked the town. Many entrenchments were dug around these ridges and some can still be seen.

In the next three and one-half years, the town was to be the scene of raid and counter-raid and was occupied many times by both armies.

For the next two years it was mainly in Union hands until April 1863 when Gen. John D. Imboden's Confederate raiders forced the Federals to withdraw. On occupying the town, Imboden reported that a third of the town had been burned by the retreating soldiers. The Confederates evacuated the town shortly afterwards and continued on their raid into the central part of the state.

Again on July 2, 1863, Confederate Gen. William L. Jackson and 1,200 men raided Beverly. The town at the time was occupied by 800 troops under Col. Thomas D. Harris. Jackson entered Randolph County by way of Valley Head and Cheat Mountain and attacked the town from three directions. One of the three columns found a still along the way and stopped to sample the brew, thus delaying the attack. Gen. William Averell marched over from Philippi, and the Southerners retreated. The Confederates lost four killed and five wounded; the Union lost 55 prisoners.

On Oct. 29, 1864, the Confederates, again under Gen. Jackson's command, coordinated an attack against Col. Robert Youart's Union command. Both armies had about the same number of men (360), but after fierce hand-to-hand combat, the Confederates were repulsed with four dead, 25 wounded and 92 captured. The Federals lost eight killed, 23 wounded and 13 captured.

The final raid of the war against the town occurred on Jan. 11, 1865 when Confederate Gen. Thomas L. Rosser, with 300 men, crossed Cheat Mountain, went down the Tygart Valley, made a detour around Beverly and formed a line of battle in a hollow within 450 yards of the Union camp.

The Union forces, again under the command of Col. Youart, had had a dance the night before, and their guard was lax. As a consequence, 580 troops were captured in their quarters, marched 162 miles over the mountains to Staunton, and put on cattle cars for the trip to Richmond and prison. Youart was subsequently dismissed from the army after this incident.

The Busrod Crawford House, the site of Gen. McClellan's headquarters and telegraph station in 1861.

The David Goff House, built in 1835. At the time of the Battle of Rich Mountain, the family fled south since Goff's sympathies lay with the South. The house was occupied by Federal troops who used it as a hospital and buried amputated limbs in the yard and garden. Soldiers' names are carved on the walls along with that of a nurse, Mary Poughkeepsie.

Logan House, site of the first amputation performed on a Union soldier, which took place on June 4, 1861. Capt. Leroy Barker Daingerfield, seriously wounded during the Battle of Philippi, was brought to this house, and Dr. John Taylor Huff, a Confederate Army doctor, was summoned from Philippi to perform the amputation. Although Dr. Huff had lost all his instruments and had to use a butcher knife to make the skin flap and a tenon saw to cut the bone, the captain recovered and lived until 1905.

The Beverly Cemetery just off Main Street, reported to be the oldest cemetery west of the Allegheny Mountains. Original graves date to 1768, but Civil War soldiers are also buried here.

The Blackman-Bosworth Store building, built about 1828 as one of the first commercial brick buildings west of the Allegheny Mountains. It was built with slave labor by David Blackman and operated as a store until the start of the war. During the war it served as a commissary. It now houses the Randolph County Museum.

The Ward home, on Ward's hill, one of three hills occupied by McClellan's army after the Rich Mountain Battle on July 11, 1861. In one night, two and one-half miles of trenches were dug. Remnants of these can still be seen around the Ward home.

A monument at Mt. Iser Cemetery, thought to be the only privately owned Confederate burial ground in the country. There are 69 soldiers and one civilian buried here on a hill overlooking Beverly. The monument was erected by the Daughters of the Confederacy in 1908 in memory of the Confederate soldiers killed in the Beverly vicinity.

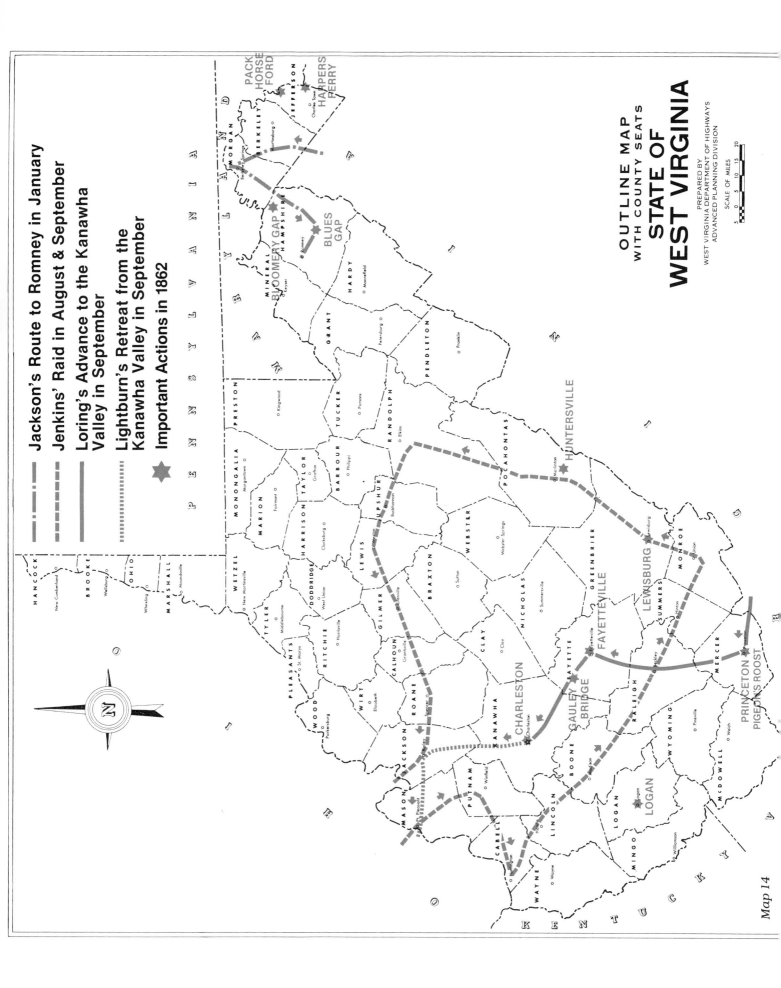

Legend:

— · — Jackson's Route to Romney in January

— — — Jenkins' Raid in August & September

———— Loring's Advance to the Kanawha Valley in September

········ Lightburn's Retreat from the Kanawha Valley in September

★ Important Actions in 1862

OUTLINE MAP
WITH COUNTY SEATS
STATE OF
WEST VIRGINIA

PREPARED BY
WEST VIRGINIA DEPARTMENT OF HIGHWAYS
ADVANCED PLANNING DIVISION

SCALE OF MILES

Map 14

1862
Consolidation

JACKSON'S CAMPAIGN

Stonewall Jackson was placed in command of the Valley District in late 1861 with headquarters in Winchester, Virginia. He wanted to clear the Federals from the district and destroy the B and O Railroad, and his first object was to capture Romney, Hampshire County. He left Winchester Jan. 1, 1862, marching first to Berkeley Springs, Morgan County and then to Hancock, Maryland, but he could not take Hancock and his troops were turned back at Blues Gap, fifteen miles east of Romney. The Union commander, thinking Jackson had an overwhelming superiority of number, evacuated Romney, however, and Jackson moved in.

Jackson considered Romney a strategic base and ordered Gen. Loring to hold the town while he returned to Winchester. There was a lot of resentment against Jackson for keeping Loring at Romney and he was accused of committing a strategic blunder. Letters were written to the Confederate secretary of war in Richmond complaining of conditions in Romney, and on Jan. 30 Loring was directed to evacuate the town in defiance of Jackson's authority. Jackson reluctantly ordered Loring back to Winchester and then wrote a letter of resignation from the army. Governor Letcher and Gen. Joseph Johnston persuaded him to withdraw his letter for the good of the Confederacy. Loring was transferred to southwest Virginia and Jackson went on to immortality.

T. J. "Stonewall" Jackson (1824-63), Confederate general, who was born in Clarksburg, Harrison County, in 1824. He commanded troops in the eastern panhandle and at Harpers Ferry in 1861-62.

View of Romney, Hampshire County, in 1862 when it was under control of Union Gen. Kelley. The town changed hands at least 56 times during the war.
Author's collection

The regimental mess of the 23 Ohio Volunteer Infantry near present-day Beckley, Raleigh County on Jan. 24, 1862. Col. R.B. Hayes is seated on the left.   RBHL

Col. Hayes witnessed a friendly sabre bout on Jan. 24, 1862. Hayes is in the center background.   RBHL

BURNING OF PRINCETON

Princeton was the county seat of Mercer County in 1862 and was one of the few towns with southern sympathies burned by the Confederates during the war. It was set afire on May 1 to keep the supplies stored there from falling into Union hands, but a Federal force under Col. Rutherford B. Hayes saved part of the town. (Lt. William McKinley served under Hayes there.) The Boone and Logan County courthouses had been burned earlier by Federal troops.

THE BATTLE OF PIGEON'S ROOST

A small battle occurred at a place called "Pigeon's Roost" because of the millions of wild pigeons that congregated there. The Confederates had occupied Princeton, county seat of Mercer County, in May 1862. Four different armies, three Confederate and one Union, were either stationed in the vicinity or closing in on Princeton.

On the night of May 16, Union Gen. Jacob Cox, stationed at Oakvale, dispatched a regiment of mostly German conscripts, commanded by Col. Von Blessing, to attack Princeton from the south.

Early on the morning of the 17th, however, Cox moved his own forces into Princeton and occupied it.

Confederate Gen. Gabriel C. Wharton, marching towards town, thought that his fellow Southerners were still there. When he reached Pigeon's Roost, one mile south of Princeton, he discovered the Union troops, but Col. Von Blessing's conscripts did not notice the Confederates.

Wharton saw a good opportunity to ambush the command, and dispatched Maj. Peter Otey with three companies of infantry and an artillery piece to hide in the tall grass at the roost.

The Germans walked right into the ambush, reportedly slightly inebriated from a captured Confederate wagon full of whiskey.

The Union troops fled down the hill to the area of the present Princeton Athletic Field and then on to Spanishburg, where they met Cox's troops who had by then evacuated Princeton.

With three Confederate armies opposed to the much smaller Union forces, the Confederates should have trapped the enemy in Princeton. But the Federals were allowed to escape because of inept Confederate commands.

Federal losses were 23 killed, 69 wounded and 21 missing. Most of the casualties were in Von Blessing's command. The Confederates lost three killed and 21 wounded.

The McNutt House at the corner of Honaker Ave. and North Walker Street in Princeton, Mercer County. The house was on fire when Federal troops entered Princeton on May 1, 1862. They put out the fire and made it their headquarters with Lt. Col. Rutherford B. Hayes in command.

Col. Rutherford B. Hayes (1822-1893) of the 23rd Ohio Volunteer Infantry. He spent considerable time in West Virginia during the war. He was elected Governor of Ohio in 1867 and President of the U.S. in 1876.   RBHL

Pvt. William McKinley (1843-1901) of Co. E, 23rd Ohio Volunteer Infantry. Probably taken at Camp Chase, Ohio before he left to serve in West Virginia. He was elected President of the United States in 1897.   W. Va. State Archives

Col. Piatt's Zouaves, the 34th Ohio Volunteer Infantry, who surprised and routed a band of Confederates between Hurricane and Logan in the winter of 1862. From the Jan. 18, 1862, issue of Harpers Weekly.
Author's Collection

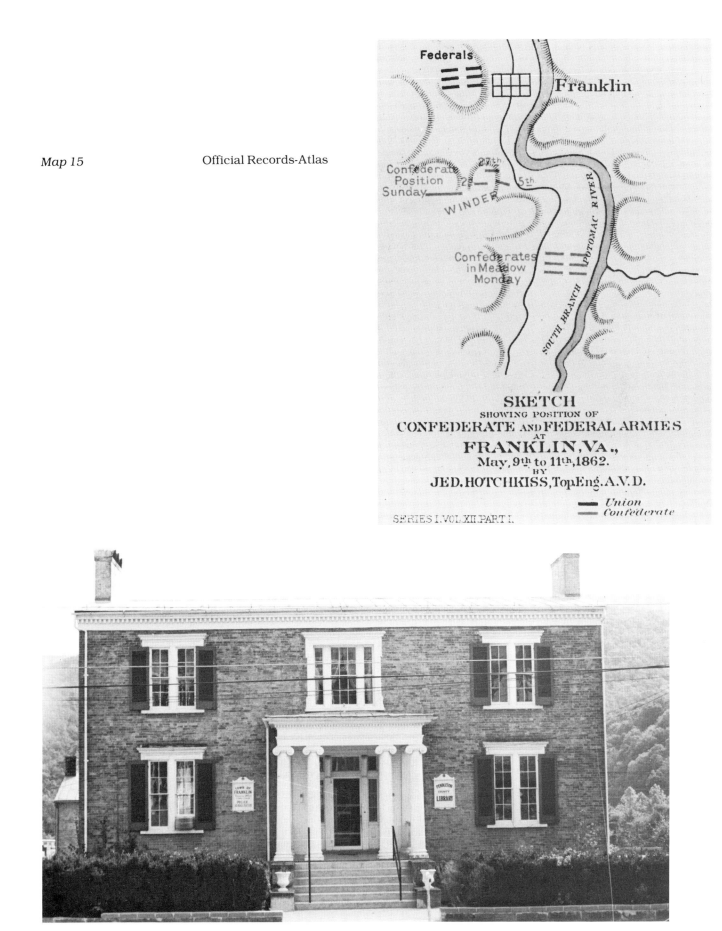

Map 15   Official Records-Atlas

Federals

Franklin

Confederate
Position
Sunday

27th

2

5th

WINDER

SOUTH BRANCH POTOMAC RIVER

Confederates
in Meadow
Monday

SKETCH
SHOWING POSITION OF
CONFEDERATE AND FEDERAL ARMIES
AT
FRANKLIN, VA.,
May, 9th to 11th, 1862.
BY
JED. HOTCHKISS, TopEng. A.V.D.

━━━ *Union*
═══ *Confederate*

SERIES I. VOL. XII. PART I.

The McCoy House on Main Street in Franklin, Pendleton County. It was constructed in 1850 with slave labor by William McCoy, an attorney and large land owner in the county. The Union Army under Gen. R.C. Schenck used the house as a communications center before and during the Battle of McDowell on May 8, 1862. It is now used as the Franklin Town Hall and Pendleton County Library.

Valley View Farm on Route 60, two miles west of Lewisburg, Greenbrier County. It was built in 1828 and known as Tuckwiller's Tavern during the war. A skirmish was fought on the grounds on May 2, 1863, and the house was used as a hospital and Union Army headquarters. The skirmish was a Union defeat.

BATTLE OF LEWISBURG

One of the most strategic towns in West Virginia was Lewisburg, Greenbrier County. It straddled the James River and Kanawha Turnpike and was the gateway to the Kanawha Valley and the Virginia Valley.

Col. George Crook, commanding Union troops, had been on a railroad raid near Covington, Virginia, when he learned that Gen. Henry Heth's Southern troops were hurrying toward him. He proceeded to Lewisburg and occupied the town on May 12. Heth attacked the town on the morning of May 23 and caught the Federal troops by surprise. However, after reforming their lines the Federals beat back the Confederates who retreated to Caldwell, a few miles west of Lewisburg, burned the covered bridge spanning the Greenbrier River, and then fled down to Monroe County.

A Revolutionary War cannon used by the Confederates was captured during the battle. It had first been captured at Yorktown in 1781 and was pressed into service again in 1861. It was sent to Springfield, Ohio, the hometown of one of the Union regiments that fought in the battle, and was placed in front of the Memorial Hall there.

Gen. Henry Heth (1825-99), Confederate Commander at the battle of Lewisburg in May 1862.
Author's Collection

The Greenbrier County Library building on Courtney Drive in Lewisburg, Greenbrier County. It was built in 1834 to house the law library of the Supreme Court of Virginia, which met in Lewisburg. During the war it served as a military hospital.

The Old Stone Presbyterian Church at Church and Foster streets in Lewisburg, Greenbrier County. It was built in 1796 and served as a military hospital during the war. It is the oldest continuously used church in this part of the state.

The John Wesley Methodist Church on East Foster Street in Lewisburg, Greenbrier County. Built in 1820, it is one of the oldest brick churches in the state. During the Battle of Lewisburg it was struck by cannon fire. Following the war it was taken over by freed slaves, and it is still in use.

Elmhurst at Caldwell, Greenbrier County, on Route 60. It was built in 1824 and used as a stage stop. A skirmish was fought here after the Battle of Lewisburg. Trenches are still visible on the property.

JENKINS RAID

Gen. Albert G. Jenkins of Cabell County led a raiding party of 550 Confederate cavalrymen from Salt Sulphur Springs in Monroe County on Aug. 24. He passed through Greenbrier, Pocahontas and Randolph Counties and after capturing the towns of Buckhannon, Weston, Glenville, Spencer and Ripley, crossed into Ohio, becoming the first Confederate to carry the rebel flag into that state. He recrossed into West Virginia below Point Pleasant, Mason County, and marched to Guyandotte and Raleigh Courthouse. His raid dramatized the inadequacy of Union defenses, weakened early in August by the transfer of 5,000 troops from the Kanawha Valley command to Gen. John Pope's army in Virginia. This raid convinced the Confederate command that they could retake the Kanawha Valley, and Gen. Loring did so in September.

Gen. Albert G. Jenkins (1830-64). Confederate general who was born in Cabell County. He was a lawyer and representative to the Confederate Congress from Charleston. He fought under Gen. Floyd in the Kanawha Valley, led a raid through central West Virginia in 1862, and was killed at the Battle of Cloyd's Mountain in 1864.

WVU Archives

KANAWHA VALLEY CAMPAIGN

In 1862 Union forces controlled the Kanawha Valley with a large supply depot at Gauley Bridge and forts at Fayetteville and other points. Gen. Joseph A.J. Lightburn from Lewis County was in command although some of his troops had been transferred to Virginia. Gen. Loring, the Confederate commander, was stationed at Pearisburg, Virginia, and Lee directed him to again invade the area, capture the Kanawha Valley and use it as a base to recover Trans-Allegheny Virginia. The salt supply at Charleston was a deciding factor in this operation, as the South was short of salt.

Loring left Sept. 1 with 4,000 troops and marched to Fayetteville. A battle there on Sept. 11 resulted in an unexpected Union rout. Lightburn ordered a general retreat and called in his outposts at Ansted and Summersville, thus opening up the entire Kanawha Valley. He retreated down the Cotton Hill road near Gauley Bridge to Marmet in Kanawha County while the main body of his troops retreated down the Kanawha Turnpike with a wagon train thirteen miles long. His army finally rejoined at Charleston for defense of the city.

Early in the morning of Sept. 13, the first units of Loring's army arrived in Charleston in the vicinity of the present university grounds. After an all-day

Brig. Gen. Joseph Andrew Jackson Lightburn (1831-1901), Commander of the Union troops who were driven from the Kanawha Valley in September 1862. WVU Archives

battle Lightburn retreated toward the Ohio River, cutting the cables on the bridge over the Elk River at Charleston. Loring did not pursue him. The Southern forces stated that they came into the Kanawha Valley not as invaders but as liberators and Loring issued this proclamation:

To the People of Western Virginia.

The Army of the Confederate States has come among you to expel the enemy, to rescue the people from the despotism of the counterfeit State Government imposed upon you by Northern bayonets, and to restore the country once more to its natural allegiance to the State. We fight for peace and the possession of our own territory. We do not intend to punish those who remain at home as quiet citizens in obedience of the laws of the land, and to all such clemency and amnesty are declared; but those who persist in adhering to the cause of the public enemy, and the pretended State Government he has erected at Wheeling, will be dealt with as their obstinate treachery deserves.

When the liberal policy of the Confederate Government shall be introduced and made known to the people, who have so long experienced the wanton misrule of the invader, the Commanding General expects the people heartily to sustain it not only as a duty, but as a deliverance from their taskmasters and usurpers. Indeed, he already recognizes in the cordial welcome which the people everywhere give to the Army, a happy indication of their attachment to their true and lawful Government.

Until the proper authorities shall order otherwise, and in the absence of municipal law and its customary ministers, Martial Law will be administered by the Army and the Provost Marshals. Private rights and property will be respected, violence will be repressed, and order promoted, and all the private property used by the Army will be paid for.

The Commanding General appeals to all good citizens to aid him in these objects, and to all able-bodied men to join his army to defend the sanctities of religion and virtue, home, territory, honor, and law, which are invaded and violated by an unscrupulous enemy, whom an indignant and united people are now about to chastise on his own soil.

The Government expects an immediate and enthusiastic response to this call. Your country has been reclaimed for you from the enemy by soldiers, many of whom are from distant parts of the State, and the Confederacy; and you will prove unworthy to possess so beautiful and fruitful a land, if you do not now rise to retain and defend it. The oaths which the invader imposed upon you are void. They are immoral attempts to restrain you from your duty to your State and Government. They do not exempt you from the obligation to support your Government and to serve in the Army; and if such persons are taken as prisoners of war, the Confederate Government guarantees to them the humane treatment of the usages of war.

By Command of
MAJ. GEN. LORING
H. Fitzhugh
Chief of Staff

The Confederate occupation did not last long. Concentrations of Federal troops at Clarksburg and Point Pleasant forced Loring to abandon the valley and retreat toward Lewisburg on Oct. 8 after originally being ordered to march on the Cheat River Bridge in Preston County. He was relieved of his command on Oct. 16 and Gen. John Echols of Monroe County took over and moved back into Charleston. He was in turn forced out of the valley Oct. 29, and the valley was in Northern hands for good. During most of the six-week occupation the Confederates concentrated on moving salt out of Kanawha Salines to eastern Virginia.

Gen. William W. Loring (1818-86), Confederate commander in the Kanawha Valley campaign of September 1862. He had lost an arm in the Mexican War. He also served under Lee in his 1861 Cheat Mountain campaign and under Gen. Stonewall Jackson at Romney in January 1862.
WVU Archives

CIVIL WAR NEWSPAPERS

During the course of the war in the state, 18 newspapers, 17 Union and one Confederate, were printed for soldiers by soldiers. Most of them were printed in established print shops vacated by the owner; a few were done on portable presses. Papers were published in Clarksburg, Lewisburg, Point Pleasant, Charles Town, Martinsburg and Charleston.

Gen. Loring had his paper, the *Guerilla,* printed in Charleston in the confiscated plant of the *Kanawha Valley Star,* but it was published for only a week, Sept. 28 to Oct. 4, 1862. The *Yankee* was printed in May 1862 by the 44th Ohio Infantry in Lewisburg on the press of the *Greenbrier Weekly Era.* Among the very few of these papers in existence today, several are in the West Virginia State Archives.

GENERAL ORDER.

HEAD QUARTERS,
DEPARTMENT OF WESTERN VIRGINIA,
Charleston, Va., Sept. 24, 1862.

General Order, No.

The money issued by the Confederate Government is secure, and is receivable in payment of public dues, and convertible into 8 per cent. bonds. Citizens owe it to the country to receive it in trade; and it will therefore be regarded as good in payment for supplies purchased for the army.

Persons engaged in trade are invited to resume their business and open their stores.

By order of

MAJ. GEN. LORING.

A general order issued by Gen. Loring during his occupation of Charleston, Kanawha County, in September 1862. W.Va. Archives

THE GUERILLA.
DEVOTED TO SOUTHERN RIGHTS AND INSTITUTIONS.

Vol. 1.   CHARLESTON, VA., OCTOBER 3, 1862.   No. 6

One of only two known issues of the Guerilla, a newspaper printed for a week when Gen. Loring's Confederate troops occupied Charleston. They took over the printing plant of the Kanawha Valley Star. W.Va. Archives

Fort Scammon, on top of Fort Hill in Charleston, Kanawha County. It was built by Union troops in 1863 to protect the city, but it was never used in battle. Future presidents Rutherford B. Hayes and William McKinley were stationed briefly at the fort. It is now owned by the City of Charleston.

CHARLESTON
Sept. 13th 1862. 34th, 37th, 44th & 47th O V I

General Lightburn's troops, shown cutting the cables of the Elk River Bridge at Charleston, Kanawha County, on their retreat from the city on Sept. 13, 1862.
Author's Collection

Ruins of the cement mill (top) and kilns (bottom) at Park Horse Ford near Shepherdstown, Jefferson County. It was built as a flour mill about 1826 and converted to a cement mill about 1829. It was partially burned by the Federals on Aug. 19, 1861 and was the scene of the Battle of Cement Mill on Sept. 20, 1862.
Tom Hahn, Shepherdstown, W.Va.

Harper's Weekly October 11, 1862

The 5th New York at Pack Horse Ford on Sept. 19, 1862. They are firing from the C & O Canal on the Maryland side towards the cement mill across the Potomac River on the West Virginia side.

Harper's Weekly, Oct. 11, 1862

Pack Horse Ford near the ruins of the cement mill, looking to the Maryland side. Lee's army crossed the Potomac here after the Battle of Antietam in September 1862.

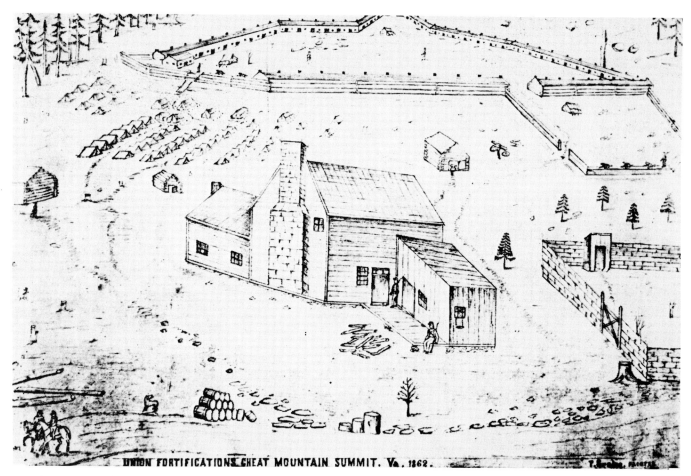

A primitive drawing of the Union fortification on Cheat Mountain Summit in 1862. This was the highest site for a Union camp during the war.

Randolph County Historical Society

Old jail at Pruntytown, Taylor County, on Route 50. The first slaves released by the order of President Lincoln were freed here on Nov. 22, 1862. The slaves were kept here to keep them from joining the Union forces, and the President declared them "contraband of war." It is now part of the West Virginia Industrial School for Boys.

A recruitment poster urging Kanawha Valley citizens to join the Union Army and drive the Rebels from the area.   WVU Archives

SOUTHERN SYMPATHIES

Illustrative of the divided loyalties of the people of the state is this order of assessment placed on Southern sympathizers by Union forces in Tucker County to compensate Union sympathizers for theft and destruction of property. This was directed to an Adam Harper:

St. George, Tucker County, Va 11/28/62

Mr. Adam Harper, Sir:

In consequence of certain roberies which have been committed upon citizens of this country by bands of Gurilies you are hereby assessed to the amount of (285.00) Two Hundred and 85 Dollars to make good their losses. And upon your failure to make good this assessment by the 8th day of Dec., the following order has been issued to me by Bridadier General R.H. Milroy:

"You are to burn their houses, seize their property and shoot them. You will be sure that you strictly carry out this order. You will require of the inhabitants for ten or fifteen miles around your camp on all the roads approaching the town upon which the enemy may approach that they must dash in and give you notice and that upon any one failing to do so you will burn their houses and shoot the men.

By order of
by Brigadier General R.H. Milroy:
Captain Kellogg Commanding 123rd Ohio

This assessment was disliked by both sides and Milroy's superiors put a stop to the practice soon afterwards.

Head Quarters,
DEPARTMENT OF SOUTH-WESTERN VIRGINIA, }
SALT SULPHUR SPRINGS, August   1862. }

GENERAL ORDERS, No.

By direction of the General Commanding is hereto appended a list of those absent without leave from the 2nd Brigade of this Command. All such absentees are ordered to report to their respective Regiments, Battalions or Companies within ten days from the publication of this order. Those so reporting within this period will be assigned to duty without further trial. Those failing to report within the prescribed limit of time will be proceeded against as deserters. The absentees from Maj. Jackson's Battalion of Cavalry will be allowed fifteen days to report.

By Order of   Maj. Gen. W. W. LORING.
August 20th, 1862.   W. B. MYERS, A. Adjt. General.

A List of Men absent from the 8th Va. Cavalry.

B. F. Aiken,	R. B. Diggs,	Andrew Greer,	William Lacy,
John P. Aiken,	Kinser,	Henry Davis,	Sampson Simmons,
J. W. Anderson,	Smith,	Stephen F. Jones,	J. B. Beckwith,
W. Anderson,	Spencer,	D. A. Taylor,	Simonton,
J. Anderson,	Coleman,	C. Wesley,	W. W. Hamilton,
D. W. Bean,	Kidd,	J. Cossett,	J. Ralsin,
J. H. Copenhaver,	Peerry,	Wm. M. Boone,	T. R. C. Blankinship,
S. M. Copenhaver,	Thornhill,	J. W. Bowyer,	W. H. Russel,
Wm. E. Copenhaver,	Fitzpatrick,	Wm. R. Thornton,	A. Hornbert,
W. W. Thompson,	Ferguson,	A. J. Woodall,	Edwin Lambert,
J. Park,	Stewart,	H. Davidson,	Paul C. Smith,
Thomas Copenhaver,	Jones,	Fletcher,	J. W. Harman,
A. B. Cook,	Staples,	Muse,	Wm. C. Sogner,
A. P. Cole,	Ballon,	A. B. Nash,	J. E. Maurice,
John J. Hester,	Spencer,	J. D. Morton,	M. B. Ranbirne,
S. T. Morrison,	Joseph Faber,	J. B. Perdue,	William Stevens,
L. G. Maupin,	H. A. Bourn,	S. W. Sinclair,	J. Strader,
J. M. Saunders,	J. D. Pickett,	Ely,	J. J. Stafford,
J. L. Thomas,	J. Austin,	Thompson,	A. T. Snyder,
James R. Evans,	William Austin,	A. P. Handley,	P. R. Snyder,
James Nuckles,	Martin Nelson,	P. M. Russel,	W. G. Panley,
Thomas Smith,	Henry Nelson,	J. V. Ralson,	J. P. Lambert,
John C. Hite,	M. Honk,	J. E. Shelton,	T. P. Hereford,
James W. Mathews,	E. W. Greer,	A. Page,	William A. Smith.

J. M. CORNS,   A. C. BAILEY,
Col. 8th Va. Cavalry.   Adjt. 8th Regt. Va. Cavalry.

D. A. ST. CLAIR'S POWER PRESS, WYTHEVILLE, VA.

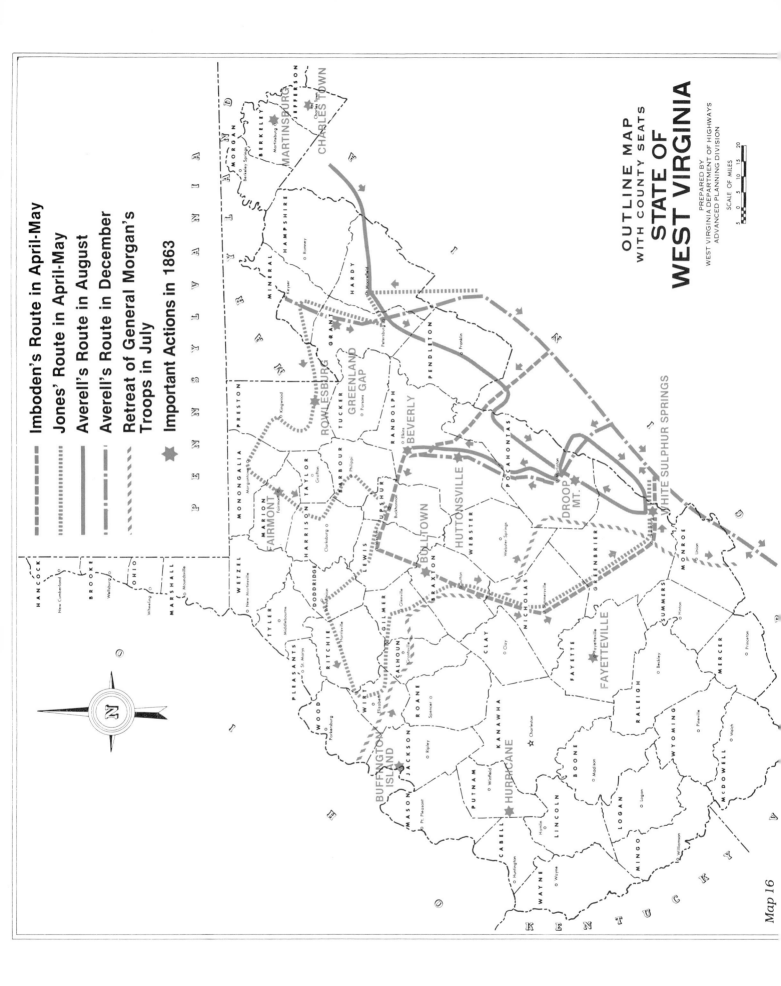

Imboden's Route in April-May

Jones' Route in April-May

Averell's Route in August

Averell's Route in December

Retreat of General Morgan's Troops in July

★ Important Actions in 1863

OUTLINE MAP
WITH COUNTY SEATS
STATE OF
WEST VIRGINIA

PREPARED BY
WEST VIRGINIA DEPARTMENT OF HIGHWAYS
ADVANCED PLANNING DIVISION

SCALE OF MILES
5   0   5   10   15   20

Map 16

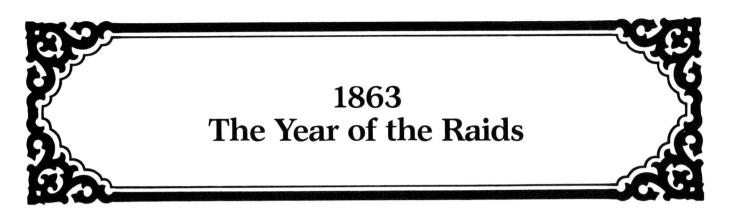

1863
The Year of the Raids

Confederate armies were riding high at the beginning of 1863 in the eastern and western theaters of war, and their successes were to continue until the twin disasters of Vicksburg and Gettysburg in July. However, in West Virginia, the Union forces had consolidated their positions and the destruction of the Virginia and Tennessee Railroad in Virginia became one of their major objectives. The Confederates had to be content with making raids to obtain supplies and disrupt the B and O Railroad.

JONES-IMBODEN RAID

Gen. Lee wrote to Gen. John D. Imboden outlining a policy of war for West Virginia and urged him to carry it out. Among other things, the municipal officers of the Reorganized Government of Virginia, called by Lee "the Pierpont government," were to be captured whenever possible, and Imboden was instructed to "render the position of sheriff as dangerous a position as possible."

The great raid of the year was conducted by Confederate Gens. Imboden and William E. Jones. Jones was the ranking officer but the plan was formulated by Imboden. He wrote Gen. Lee outlining plans for a raid to destroy the B and O Railroad from Oakland, Maryland, to Grafton; defeat the enemy at Beverly, Philippi and Buckhannon; recruit for the Confederate army and control the northwest part of the state to enable the people to take part in the Virginia state elections in May. Except for the partial destruction of the railroad and the capture of thousands of horses and cattle, the raid was of little benefit to the Confederacy.

Lee split the raiders into two independent groups commanded by Jones and Imboden, but the forces were to join later. Imboden left Shenandoah Moun-

The site of the first oil well drilled in West Virginia. Located on State Route 5 at Burning Springs, Wirt County, the well was drilled in 1860 and in 1863 was the target of the Jones-Imboden Raid, the first instance of oil field destruction in warfare.
HPU

JONES-IMBODEN RAID

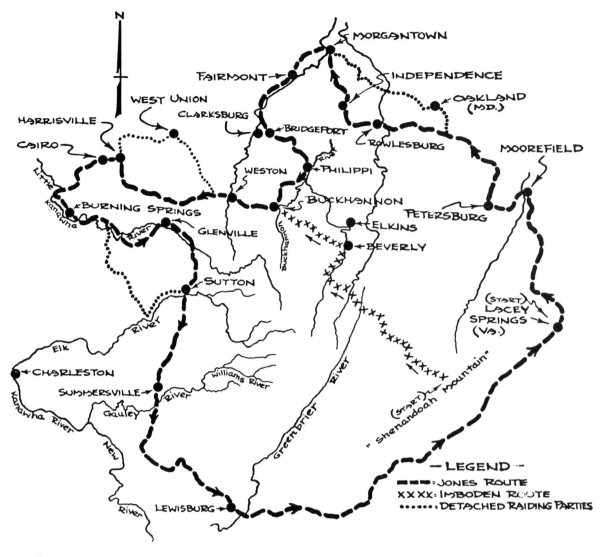

Map 17

tain near Staunton, Virginia, with 3,400 infantry on April 20, 1863. He marched to Beverly and then to Buckhannon, Upshur County, which he occupied April 29 and waited for Jones to meet him. His main objectives were Grafton and Clarksburg, but they were too strongly defended to be attacked.

Jones left Lacey Springs, Virginia, on April 21 with 1,300 men. He marched through Moorefield and Petersburg and fought a battle at Greenland Gap in Grant County. On April 26 he attacked Rowlesburg in Preston County in a bid to destroy the B and O Railroad trestles across the Cheat River. He could not accomplish this and thus one of the main objectives of the raid was not carried out. His troops marched to Morgantown, Monongalia County, took the town and then proceeded to Fairmont, Marion County, where they destroyed the large iron railroad bridge across the Monongahela River. He bypassed Clarksburg and Grafton, marched to Philippi and found Imboden at Buckhannon. They planned to capture Clarksburg, a large Federal supply depot, and moved to Weston, Lewis County for the attack. But Clarksburg was still too strongly defended, so

Imboden moved on to Summersville, Nicholas County.

Jones left Weston on May 6 and passed through West Union and Cairo via the Parkersburg pike in an effort to cut the Northwestern Virginia Railroad. On May 9 he swung toward "Oiltown" (Burning Springs in Wirt County) and his troops went up the hollows and ravines and put the torch to oil storage tanks and loaded barges on the Little Kanawha River and Burning Springs Run. The whole countryside was ablaze and 150,000 barrels of oil went up in smoke. This was the first burning of an oil installation in the history of warfare.

Jones drove an estimated 3,000 cattle and over 1,200 horses through Beverly over the Parkersburg and Staunton Turnpike into Virginia. They were captured in Marion and Harrison counties. It was the largest drove of livestock ever to pass along the road.

The two separate forces were united at Summersville on May 14 and made their way back to the security of the Confederate lines in the Shenandoah Valley.

The old and new Cheat River Bridge at Macomber, Preston County, on Route 50. The covered one, built in 1835 and burned down in 1964, was used by both armies during the war. On April 27, 1863, Confederate Gen. Jones's army passed over the bridge and tore up the decking on one side. It took two years to repair. This photo was taken in the 1930s.
Author's Collection

The Cheat River Covered Bridge piers, still intact at Macomber.

Barracksville Covered Bridge at Barracksville, Marion County. It was built in 1854 by the Chenoweth Brothers and was saved from destruction by local residents pleading with Confederate General Jones who passed by here on April 29, 1863.

BATTLE OF HURRICANE BRIDGE

A large Federal supply depot was located at Point Pleasant, Mason County. Confederate Gen. Albert Jenkins, who commanded a cavalry brigade at Dublin, decided to mount a raid across the mountains and down the Kanawha Valley, a distance of more than 200 miles, to capture the town and supplies. He left Dublin on March 20, 1863, with 800 men and a week later reached Hurricane Bridge, Putnam County. A Federal force was stationed here, blocking the way to Point Pleasant.

On the 28th, the Confederates delivered a note demanding an unconditional surrender of the enemy force. The Federals refused the demand, and for the next five hours there was heavy fire from both sides. The Confederates then withdrew and resumed their march towards Point Pleasant. The Federals reported several casualties; none was reported on the Confederate side.

Site of the Battle of Hurricane Bridge near Hurricane, Putnam County, on Route 60. Union forces stationed here were attacked by Confederates and withdrew to Point Pleasant after a five-hour battle on March 28, 1863.

INDIRECT ARTILLERY FIRE

Indirect artillery fire was used for the first time in modern warfare at Fayetteville, Fayette County, on May 19, 1863. Sgt. Milton Humphreys placed his Confederate artillery battery behind a clump of trees and arched his shells over a hill into the fort while an observer on a hill directed his fire. Sixty-nine shells dropped into the fort, and the Union troops thought they had come from the sky. His subsequent publications on artillery methods were accepted as authoritative throughout the world. Humphreys, who was born in Greenbrier County and had lived in Sutton, became a professor of Greek and taught at several universities during his long career which lasted until his death in 1928.

Cha͞s Riedel, Camp H. 12 ᵗʰ O.V.I.   *Lithographed by Ehrgott Forbriger*

Camp of the 12 ᵗʰ Regᵗ O.V.I. at Fayetteville Va. April 1863.
A. Fort Scammon. — B. Battery Mc.Mullan.— C. Camp of the 12.Regᵗ O.VI.—D. Fayetteville Courthouse.

Camp of the 12th Regiment O.V.I. at Fayetteville, Fayette County, in April 1863.   WVU Archives

Remains of Fort Scammon can still be found within the city limits of Fayetteville. This is probably one of the trenches that surrounded the fort as shown in the top sketch.

A drawing of the last attack on Fayetteville, Fayette County on May 19, 1863, by troops under Gen. McCausland. The Confederates retreated after two days of bombarding the town.   WVU Archives

GENERAL MORGAN'S RAID

One of the most bizarre raids of the year was Confederate Gen. John Morgan's strike across Indiana and Ohio and into West Virginia in July. He had been ordered into Kentucky to repel a Union invasion but disobeyed orders. As he rode through the Indiana and Ohio countryside with his 2,400 troops, he burned railroads and military supplies and threw the population into panic. The West Virginia Legislature was in session in Wheeling and it adjourned to form a military company of mainly older men to fight the expected invader.

Morgan arrived at Buffington Island just north of Ravenswood, Jackson County, on July 18. His troops had traveled sixteen days and they were sick and worn out. The river had risen several feet and they could not cross against enemy opposition. Federal troops came from as far away as Fayette County to capture him. Two Union gunboats in West Virginia waters fired on the Confederate troops and forced Morgan up the Ohio River opposite Bellville, Wood County, where some of the men swam to the West Virginia shore. Morgan finally surrendered at Salineville, near East Liverpool, Ohio, on July 26. Some of his men retreated across West Virginia to safety in Virginia on one of the longest retreats of the war. The Buffington Island battle was the only battle fought in Ohio during the war.

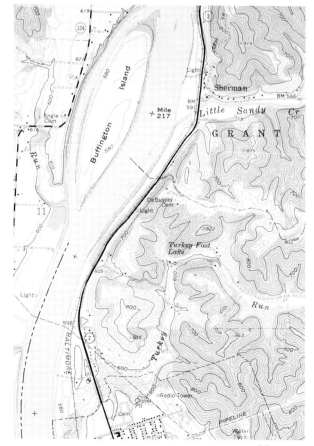

Map 18

Buffington Island in the Ohio River just north of Ravenswood, Jackson County. This was the scene on July 19, 1863 of the only battle fought in Ohio. It was fought against Morgan's Raiders, and the gunboats which took part in the battle were in West Virginia territory.

BATTLE OF WHITE SULPHUR SPRINGS

White Sulphur Springs is the site of a famous health spa and was the scene of a battle on Aug. 26 between 1,300 Union troops commanded by Gen. Averell and 2,000 Confederate troops under Col. Patton. Averell was directed to seize the law books at the Virginia State Law Library at Lewisburg, Greenbrier County, which were housed there for the convenience of the judges and lawyers at the Virginia Supreme Court of Appeals.

Averell left Winchester, Virginia, Aug. 5 and destroyed the saltpeter works at Franklin, Pendleton County. He marched to Warm Springs, Virginia, and then turned west toward Lewisburg on the James River Pike. The Confederates had marched down Anthony's Creek Road to intercept the Union force and the two armies met where the two roads intersected. The battle lasted all day and into the next. Both sides were running low on ammunition and Averell was forced to retreat when his gave out. He returned to Beverly by way of Huntersville and Marlinton in Pocahontas County. Casualties were high on both sides, and among the dead was Capt. Paul Von Konig, a German baron who was serving as aide-de-camp to Averell. Some say he was shot by his own troops. The wounded on both sides were cared for at the health spa hotel in White Sulphur Springs.

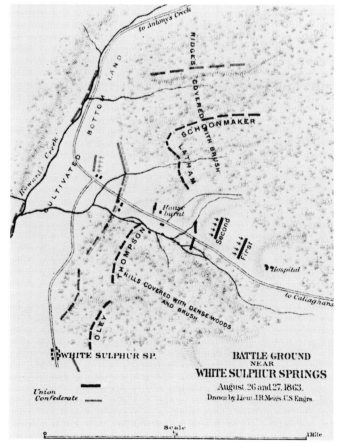

BATTLE GROUND
NEAR
WHITE SULPHUR SPRINGS
August 26 and 27, 1863.
Drawn by Lieut. J.R.Meigs U.S Engrs.

Map 19

A monument erected on the White Sulphur Springs battlefield site in 1914 by descendants of Union Capt. Baron Paul Von Konig, who was killed here on Aug. 26, 1863.

Site of the Battle of White Sulphur Springs, Dry Creek, Rocky Gap or Howard's Creek on Aug. 26 and 27, 1863, at the intersection of Routes 60 and 92. Greenbrier County. The large stone monument was erected in 1938 to commemorate Greenbrier County's 160th anniversary. Both monuments were moved to this site when the road was relocated. Most of the battlefield is now covered by a large store and parking lot.

CHARLES TOWN ATTACK

Gen. Imboden's infantry marched 48 miles in one day to attack Charles Town, Jefferson County, on Oct. 18. He captured more than 400 Union troops and then retreated. He beat Napoleon's record of marching 36 miles in one day to fight a battle.

BATTLE OF BULLTOWN

Bulltown, in Braxton County, was the scene of a battle on Oct. 13 and 14, 1863, and the Union victory helped maintain Northern control in central West Virginia. A fort had been constructed in the vicinity of the covered bridge over the Little Kanawha River. It guarded the important Weston and Gauley Bridge Turnpike.

On the 13th, Confederate Col. William L. (Mudwall) Jackson reached the fort, which had been strongly fortified by Federals in September. Jackson had been sent from the Greenbrier Valley to Bulltown to capture the fort and cut communications with the Kanawha Valley from the north. He had in his command 700 infantry, 75 cavalry and 2 artillery pieces.

Union Capt. William Mattingly had 400 men guarding the fort, but he had no artillery.

Reaching the Little Kanawha at Falls Mills on the evening of the 12th, Jackson planned to divide his command in two detachments and converge on the fort at daybreak. The attack commenced on schedule, and after a time Jackson sent an ultimatum of surrender to Mattingly. The Union commander sent back a challenge to "come and take us." A second surrender ultimatum was sent, to which the commander replied that he would "fight until hell froze over," and if he had to retreat, he would "retreat on the ice." The Confederates finally left the battlefield that night. The following day, Union reinforcements arrived, and Jackson's troops retreated into Webster County. Losses were small, with seven killed on the Confederate side and none on the Union side.

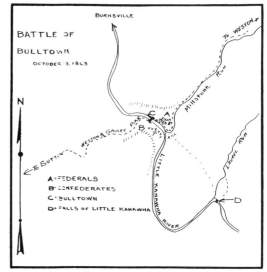

Map 20   West Virginia Review, June 1933

The Cunningham Farm near the site of the Battle of Bulltown. The Corps of Engineers has created a Civil War park here with a visitor's center, restored trenches and markers.

BATTLE OF DROOP MOUNTAIN

One of the most important battles to take place in West Virginia, and the last large-scale battle fought in the state, took place at Droop Mountain in the southern part of Pocahontas County on Nov. 6. The Confederates were under Gen. John Echols of Monroe County and the Union force was led by Gen. Averell. It was brother against brother again, with many West Virginia troops on each side. Casualties were high on both sides.

The Confederates had control of the entire Greenbrier River Valley and the Union command wanted to clear them out and strike for the Virginia and Tennessee Railroad to the south. It was hoped this move would relieve the Union forces in Tennessee who had been defeated at the Battle of Chickamauga in September. Averell left Beverly and Gen. Alfred Duffie left Charleston in a pincer movement to clear the valley. Echols was stationed at Lewisburg but had troops scattered throughout the valley.

Because of delays of the two Union columns, Echols had time to concentrate what forces he could gather on top of Droop Mountain guarding the road south to Lewisburg. This site was to become the highest battle in elevation of the Civil War. Echols had only about 1,700 men to oppose Averell's 3,000 to 4,000 troops, but the terrain was in his favor. He did not fortify his position or protect his flanks, however, and these failures cost him the battle. The Federals turned the Confederate flank and forced them to retreat through Lewisburg into Virginia. Gen. Duffie tried to get to Lewisburg ahead of the retreating army to cut it off but was not successful.

Although the Southerners were beaten, they did keep their army intact and saved the railroad from destruction. Ten days later the Confederates reoccupied many areas of the Greenbrier Valley.

Gen. John Echols (1823-96). Born in Virginia but lived and practiced law in Union, Monroe County. Succeeded Gen. Loring in October 1862 as Commander of Confederate troops in the Kanawha Valley. Commander at the Battle of Droop Mountain and fought with Gen. Early in the 1864 Shenandoah Valley campaign. After Lee's surrender he escorted President Jefferson Davis on his flight from Richmond.

Author's Collection

Droop Mountain Battlefield on Route 219 in Pocahontas County. It was the scene of a battle on Nov. 6, 1863.

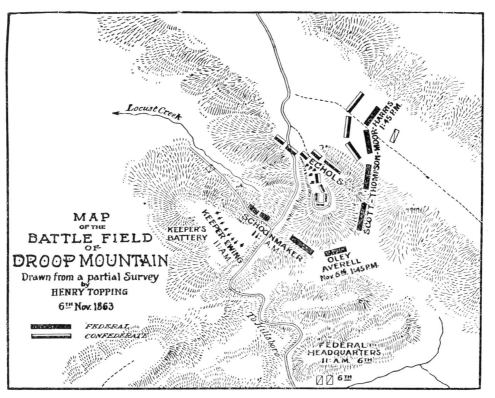

Map 21   Official Records-Atlas

GENERAL AVERELL'S SALEM RAID

Once again Gen. Averell was called upon to attack the Virginia and Tennessee Railroad, this time to relieve Gen. Ambrose Burnside who was besieged in Knoxville, Tenn. The railroad was a vital link in the southern supply system to Tennessee.

On Dec. 1, 1863, Averell ordered Gen. Eliahim Parker Scammon to take his third division via Lewisburg and Union to destroy the New River Bridge in Virginia. The first division under Gen. Jeremiah Sullivan was to cross over to Harrisonburg, Va., move down the valley and threaten Staunton.

Gen. Averell left Keyser (New Creek) on Dec. 8 in a four-mile column to Monterey and then down to Sweet Springs and New Castle just over the Virginia line. His objective was the important railroad and supply town of Salem near present-day Roanoke.

He managed to destroy the railroad four miles east and six miles west to Salem and to destroy three supply depots in town. The Confederates tried to rush troops to meet him but did not arrive in time to save the massive quantities of corn, wheat, oats, meat, leather, salt, clothing, cotton, shoes, tar, saddles and 100 wagons that were stored in Salem.

Averell left Salem after the Dec. 16 raid and camped at Catawba and Roanoke Red Sulphur Springs. On his retreat back into West Virginia, he had to avoid more than 12,000 enemy troops, cross many swollen rivers and survive freezing temperatures. He captured a dispatch and learned that only the road leading across the mountains into Pocahontas County was open. In his eight-day raid, one of the most successful of the war, he marched his army more than 400 miles and lost only 138 men.

Although the railroad was repaired in four days, the raid nevertheless dealt a devastating blow to the South.

Gen. William Averell (1832-1900), Commander of Union forces at the Battle of Droop Mountain and Moorefield. He led several raids in West Virginia and Virginia, the most notable being the raid on Salem, in December 1863.

Author's Collection

-103-

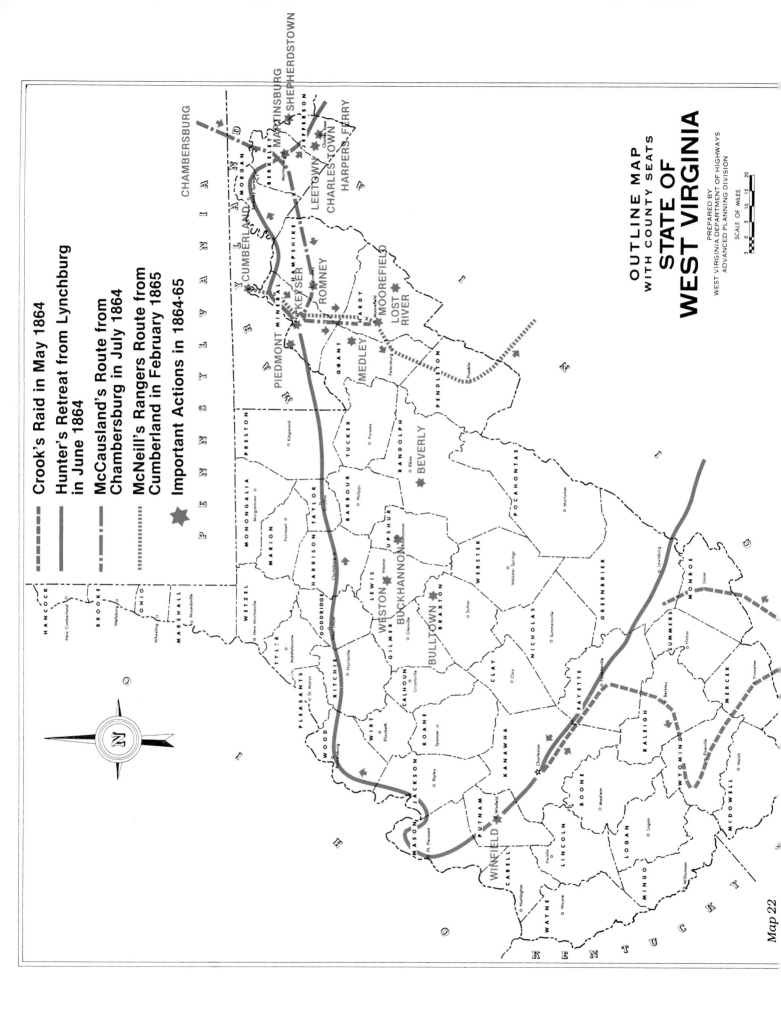

Crook's Raid in May 1864

Hunter's Retreat from Lynchburg
in June 1864

McCausland's Route from
Chambersburg in July 1864

McNeill's Rangers Route from
Cumberland in February 1865

Important Actions in 1864-65

OUTLINE MAP
WITH COUNTY SEATS
STATE OF
WEST VIRGINIA

PREPARED BY
WEST VIRGINIA DEPARTMENT OF HIGHWAYS
ADVANCED PLANNING DIVISION

SCALE OF MILES
0 5 10 15 20

Map 22

1864-65
Last Actions of the War

The last year and a half of war was mainly a period of raid and counter-raid in West Virginia with most of the larger skirmishes taking place in the eastern panhandle area. By this time the Federal forces had secured most of the new state and it was mainly a matter of keeping the "rebs" in their place and guarding the B and O Railroad. Guerrilla activity, however, continued right up until the end of the war.

Gen. John C. Breckenridge had assumed command of Confederate forces in West Virginia in March 1864, while Gen. David Hunter took over command of Union forces in May 1864.

CROOK'S RAID

One of the largest Union raids of 1864 was Gen. George Crook's drive into Virginia to try to destroy the salt works at Saltville and to cut and destroy as much as he could of the vital Virginia and Tennessee Railroad. He was to coordinate his attack with Gen. Franz Sigel, who was to leave Martinsburg and travel up the Shenandoah Valley to meet Crook at Staunton, Virginia. Sigel was defeated soundly at the Battle of New Market, Virginia, on May 15, however, and Crook was on his own.

Crook left Charleston on May 2, 1864, and traveled through Gauley Bridge, Fayetteville, Beckley, Oceania and Princeton into Virginia. He met a Confederate force under Gen. Albert G. Jenkins at Cloyd's Mountain near Dublin, Virginia, on May 9 and defeated it. Gen. Jenkins was killed in this engagement. This was mainly a battle between West Virginia troops on both sides and both had scores to settle. The Union cavalry under Gen. Averell had gone in another direction and managed to destroy part of the railroad but not the salt works. Both Union commands met afterwards at Union, Monroe County, and went to Meadow Bluff to rest before returning to the Kanawha Valley.

GENERAL HUNTER

After the New Market battle, Gen. Hunter marched his Union army against Lynchburg, Staunton and Lexington, Virginia. At Lynchburg on June 17 he met strong resistance and thinking that Confederate Gen. Jubal Early's troops had

arrived he retreated through Sweet Springs and Lewisburg, down the Kanawha River to the Ohio, and up to Parkersburg, where he entrained to Martinsburg to try again to stop Gen. Early's army. His retreat through the state had lasted a week and portions of a letter from one of his soldiers shows how the men fared in the mountains of West Virginia —

On and on we went; at last we halted. Of course we did not pitch our tents. We had dispensed with almost everything of that kind long ago. Our clothes were fast passing away. Many had worn out their shoes and were barefoot. Everything that was eatable that came in our way was eaten, such as roots and herbs. We pealed the black birch trees and ate the bark. I crippled along, stopping when I could go no farther. I thought of leaving my equipment and breaking my Springfield but finally brought them through. Their weight was about 18 pounds and they were all that we had to protect ourselves. Rations came in just before dark. The mountains ring and echo back the shouts of joy. Cheer on Cheer on now went up until we were hoarse and out of breath.

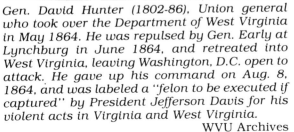

Gen. David Hunter (1802-86), Union general who took over the Department of West Virginia in May 1864. He was repulsed by Gen. Early at Lynchburg in June 1864, and retreated into West Virginia, leaving Washington, D.C. open to attack. He gave up his command on Aug. 8, 1864, and was labeled a "felon to be executed if captured" by President Jefferson Davis for his violent acts in Virginia and West Virginia.

WVU Archives

At White Sulphur Springs, Greenbrier County, on June 24, Gen. Hunter decided to burn the famous health spa hotel but was convinced by Capt. Henry A. duPont of the famous duPont family to save the buildings in case the Union forces came through again and needed them. Hunter was also thwarted in another burning in July at Martinsburg. He had ordered the burning of three homes in the eastern panhandle region in retaliation for the Confederate burning of the home of the Maryland governor. Two homes were destroyed and Boydville in Martinsburg was to be the third. Mrs. Charles Faulkner, the owner of the house, pleaded with President Lincoln, and minutes before the burning a telegram was received from him sparing the house.

Rutherford B. Hayes, who fought in West Virginia during most of the war and later became president of the United States, gave his impressions of Gen. Hunter and the "rebels" in a letter he wrote home from Charleston on July 24, 1864:

Dearest:

Back again to this point last night. Camped opposite the lower end of Camp White on the broad level bottom in the angle between Elk and Kanawha. My headquarters on one of the pretty wooded hills near Judge Summer's·.

You wrote one thoughtless sentence complaining of Lincoln for failing to protect our unfortunate prisoners by retaliation. All a mistake, darling. All such things should be avoided as much as possible. We have done too much rather than too little. Gen. Hunter turned Mrs. Governor Letcher and daughter out of their home at Lexington and on 10 minutes notice burned the beautiful place in retaliation for some bushwackers' burning out Governor Pierpont (of loyal Va.). And I am glad to say that Gen. Crook's division officers and men were all disgusted with it...

You use the phrase "brutal Rebels." Don't be cheated in that way. There are enough "brutal Rebels" no doubt, but we have brutal officers on this raid. And there are plenty of humane Rebels. I have seen a good deal of it on this trip. War is a cruel business and there is brutality in it on all sides, but it is very idle to get up anxiety on account of any supposed peculiar cruelty on the part of Rebels. Keepers of prisons in Cincinnati, as well as in Danville, are hard-hearted and cruel....

*Affectionately
R.*

The resort hotel at White Suphur Springs in this 1857 rendering by Edward Beyer. This was one of the most popular resorts in the country before the war and was saved from destruction by Gen. Hunter's orders in 1864. Wounded were cared for in the main hotel after the Battle of White Sulphur Springs.

W. Va. Archives

GENERAL McCAUSLAND

Gen. John McCausland of Mason County, who had taken over command at Cloyd's Mountain after Gen. Jenkins' death, became famous in July 1864 for his raid on Chambersburg, Pennsylvania. He was directed to raid Pennsylvania in retaliation for Gen. Hunter's operations in the Shenandoah Valley. He demanded a large ransom from the town and when he did not receive it he looted and burned it. He then retreated to West Virginia and stopped in the vicinity of Romney. Being flushed with victory, he decided to expand his raid and attack Keyser (New Creek) in Mineral County, and the B and O Railroad clear to the Ohio River, and then proceed to the Kanawha Valley before heading back to the east. His attempt at Keyser failed and he retreated back to Old Fields, just north of Moorefield, where he was defeated on Aug. 7 by Gen. Averell, who had been in pursuit of him from Pennsylvania. Averell captured 420 prisoners and 400 horses and re-took the plunder from Chambersburg.

A broadside issued for men of the 5th Virginia Infantry Regiment in camp at Kanawha Falls, Fayette County, in 1864. The bottom caption states: Gives each of us a copy of this engraving, to show our friends the way we sing and hold meetings in camp. He desires us to tell them to pray for us and him, that we may prove faithful to our country and our God, and not found wanting in any day of temptation and trial.
WVU Archives

"CLAWHAMMER" WITCHER RAID

Col. Vincent A. "Clawhammer" Witcher of the 34th Battalion of Virginia Cavalry left Lewisburg on Sept. 22, 1864 to buy or capture all the horses he could to take back to eastern Virginia. On Sept. 25 he captured Bulltown and the next day Weston, then he camped a few miles from Buckhannon on the Little Kanawha Turnpike. The local citizens tried without much success to bushwhack and ambush his command, but he took Buckhannon and captured 100 troops of Union Maj. T.F. Lang's 3rd Virginia Cavalry. He destroyed many arms and supplies and took many horses back to Virginia.

BATTLE OF WINFIELD

Although the Kanawha Valley was fairly well secured by 1864, a Federal force under Capt. John Reynolds was sent to Winfield, Putnam County, in October to occupy the town and give protection to river transportation. They constructed trenches in town and around the site of the present courthouse. A Confederate force under Col. John Witcher, stationed at Mud River, south of Winfield, upon hearing of the occupation, decided to attack the town. The attack was carried out on the night of Oct. 26, 1864, by 400 men divided into two groups. One of the groups penetrated the center of the defenses in town but was forced back and the commanding officer was mortally wounded. The entire command then withdrew back to its Mud River base.

Maj. Gen. Jubal Early, Confederate commander who operated in the 1864 Shenandoah Valley campaign that threatened Washington, D.C. Some of the action took place in the eastern panhandle of the new state of West Virginia.
Harpers Ferry Bookstore

McNEILL'S RANGERS

Capt. McNeill and a small group of his McNeill's Rangers, a local band of Southern partisans operating out of Hardy County, slipped into Cumberland, Maryland, on the night of February 21 in the midst of 3,500 Union troops and captured Gens. Crook and Kelley in their hotel rooms. They slipped across the Potomac River, proceeded towards Moorefield through hundreds of enemy troops and after three days and more than 154 miles arrived in Harrisonburg, Virginia. The captured generals were sent by coach to Staunton to meet Gen. Early.

At the end of the war, the few Confederate troops left in the state laid down their arms. McNeill's Rangers surrendered at Romney in April but surrendered only their old antique firearms and kept their good weapons. They were also allowed to keep the U.S. Army cavalry saddles that they had captured and used in the war. One partisan wanted to know if he could keep a little powder to go coon hunting, or maybe to hunt a Swamp Dragon (Union home guard) along the North Fork.

The last skirmish of the war occurred on the Greenbrier Pines, seven miles east of Hinton, Summers County at Big Rock in the latter part of April 1865. Thurmond's Rangers, floating down the river in a large canoe, were fired on by Union troops from the bank. There were no casualties.

West Virginia had not heard the last. After the war, Virginia officially protested the loss of Berkeley and Jefferson counties in the eastern panhandle. The dispute went to the U.S. Supreme Court, which ruled in 1870 that these two counties should permanently remain in West Virginia.

OTHER ACTIONS IN 1864

In other parts of the state there was also considerable action. In March, Union troops destroyed the nitrate plant above Franklin, Pendleton County. On May 4, Capt. Jesse McNeill with 61 Confederate cavalrymen captured Piedmont, Mineral County, burning two trains, the machine shops and capturing 104 prisoners. Harpers Ferry was again attacked by Confederates on July 4. They besieged the town for four days, but the heavy guns on the heights drove them back and shelled them to a distance of four miles.

Much of the fighting in the eastern panhandle in the late summer was a result of Gen. Jubal Early's Shenandoah Valley campaign which threatened Washington, D.C., in an attempt to draw troops away from the Union seige around Petersburg, Va. The famous Confederate guerrilla leader John Mosby was also active in this area during the year.

Sycamore Dale on Route 28 north of Romney, Hampshire County. It was built between 1836 and 1839. Col. Lew Wallace, author of Ben Hur, *reportedly used the house as his headquarters. McNeill's Rangers surrendered to Federal troops here in 1865.*

Blue Sulphur Springs in 1859. Just prior to the war this famous health resort was turned into a Baptist College. During the war, the spa was used by both armies as a hospital. In the winter of 1862-63, several hundred Georgia troops were encamped here. Eighty-nine of them died of a typhoid fever epidemic and were buried on top of the hill in coffins made out of benches from the cottages and buildings of the resort. In 1864 Union troops burned down the rest of the buildings.   Virginia State Archives

All that remains of the famous old spa at Blue Sulphur Springs, Greenbrier County, is this Greek style springhouse in the middle of the field.

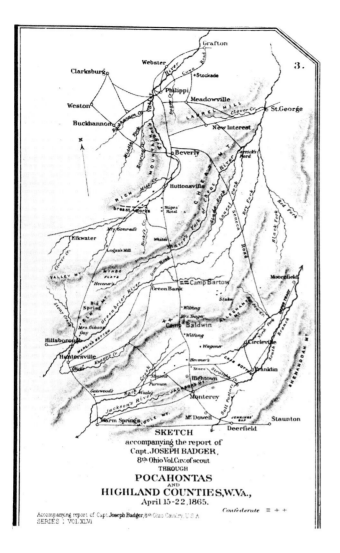

Map 23
Notice that this map places Highland County in West Virginia rather than Virginia.

Site of Fort Moore at Glenville, Gilmer County. It is on a hill behind Glenville State College and was built by the Gilmer Home Guards. Confederate troops burned it in December 1864.

KEYSER (NEW CREEK)

Keyser (New Creek) is located on the North Branch of the Potomac River on the mainline of the Baltimore and Ohio Railroad in western Mineral County. It was an important military base during the war.

Fort Fuller, now the site of Potomac State College, was built by the Union Army in 1861. It commanded roads leading to the South Branch and Shenandoah valleys and to Romney, Petersburg, Moorefield, Franklin and Winchester, Va. Fort Piano was built on top of a steep mountain just east of town.

Cannon were placed all over town, and thousands of troops were trained here. A permanent garrison with cavalry was maintained throughout the war to guarantee the important railroad line.

Gen. William Averell's great raid on Salem, Va. in December 1863 was launched from here and the troops returned here after the raid. A small engagement took place here on Aug. 4, 1864 when Confederate troops under Gen. Bradley T. Johnson and Gen. John McCausland attacked the town but were repulsed.

The major engagment of the war in the area occurred on Nov. 28, 1864 when a Confederate force under Gen. Thomas Rosser, wearing captured Union uniforms, managed to enter Fort Fuller and capture 400 troops and a great quantity of supplies. Most of the warehouses were burned at a loss of $33,000. Supplies taken by the Confederates were of great help to them, especially this late in the war. The quantities seized were quite impressive, as this list shows:

225 hats
160 dress coats
1200 trousers (cavalry)
400 blouses (coats)
150 pairs of drawers
2000 pair of stockings
250 knap sacks
300 canteens
100 spades
100 camp kettles
50 hatchets
23 guidons
500 shelter tents
54 Sibley tent stoves
8 hospital tents
76 single sets of horse and mule harnesses (worn)
100 axes
750 Great Coats (Cavalry & Infantry)
300 caps (kepis)
1400 uniform jackets
500 trousers (infantry)
1500 flannel shirts
500 pairs of boots
300 woolen blankets
250 rubber blankets
250 haversacks
100 shovels
100 mess pans
4 camp colors
4 wall tents
350 pick axes & handles
150 Company & Regimental Books
4 four-horse wagons
21 two-horse wagons
3 ambulances
39 mules
118 horses, all serviceable
169 horses, unfit for service
25 tons of hay
1600 bushels of grain

A view of Keyser, Mineral County in May 1865. The photo was taken by George Parsons and shows the camp of the 22nd Pennsylvania (Ringgolds).

WVU Archives

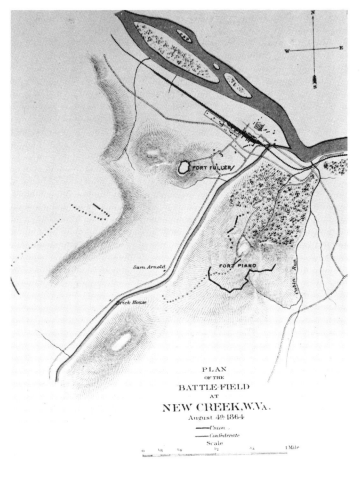

PLAN
OF THE
BATTLE-FIELD
AT
NEW CREEK, W.VA.
August 4th 1864

Scale

Map 24
New Creek is present-day Keyser, Mineral County.
Official Records-Atlas

The Potomac State College administration building now sits on the site of Fort Fuller at Keyser, Mineral County.

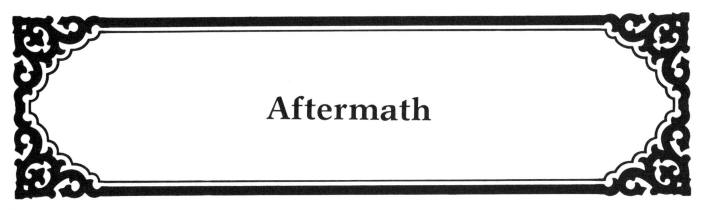

Aftermath

With Lee's surrender at Appomattox on April 9, 1865, the war was essentially over in West Virginia. McNeill's Rangers surrendered on May 8 near Romney, and this ended the bitter and violent partisan activity that had split the state during the war.

On June 1, Col. Wesley Owens left Clarksburg with 400 men and made a twelve-day expedition through Pocahontas and Pendleton counties. Part of his mission was to hunt for Virginia's Governor William Smith, who had not surrendered to Federal authorities. He was also to collect government property, mostly horses, scattered through the area. No trace was found of the fugitive governor.

Col. Owens noted that the country was exhausted and desolated. Only two families were found in Huntersville, Pocahontas County. The paroled Confederate soldiers were coming home to try to rebuild their lives. By the terms of surrender, the defeated soldiers who had horses or mules were permitted to keep them to help with the spring planting at home.

Although the state was saved from the ravages and inequalities that the reconstruction period imposed on the vanquished Confederacy, it took many years for bitter feelings to subside in this border state.

Through the years there was a proliferation of monuments erected to the dead of both sides in many counties of the state, but there seem to be more Confederate than Union monuments. Veterans' organizations were established in the state, the Grand Army of the Republic for Union veterans and the United Confederate Veterans for the Confederates, along with their auxiliary units. Reunions were held through the years to keep alive memories of what was probably the high point in the lives of many of the men of both sides.

To illustrate the deep division that occurred in the state during the war, records show that at the 50th anniversary reunion of the Battle of Gettysburg in July 1913, West Virginia was the only state to have an almost equal number of veterans from both sides attending (approximately 360).

It was truly brother against brother in this part of the country.

Pocahontas County Confederate veterans off for a reunion in Richmond in 1907.
Pocahontas County Historical Society

Members of the Logan County Wildcats, Co. D, 36th Va. Infantry, Confederate Army, gather for a reunion, probably in Logan. Date unknown.   Terry Lowry

An 1893 view of the reunion of Capt. Albert Jenkins' Border Rangers, Co. E Va. Calvary. Most of these men fought at Scary Creek in 1861.   James E. Marrow Library, Marshall University

McNeill's Rangers reunion at Moorefield, Hardy County on Aug. 31, 1910.   Hardy County Library

Reunion of the 23rd Ohio Volunteer Infantry Regiment who spent considerable time in West Virginia during the war. The reunion took place at Lakeside, Ohio in the 1880s.   RBHL

Gen. John McCausland and his daughter, Charlotte, probably taken at their home in Mason County in the early 1900s. McCausland died in 1927, the last remaining Confederate general.

Mike Price-South Hills Antiques, Charleston

General Robert E. Lee and friends at White Sulphur Springs in 1869. According to the now accepted identifications, subjects seated in the photograph, commencing from the left, are 1)Blacque Bey, Turkish Minister to the United States, 1867 to 1873; 2) General Lee; 3) George Peabody of Massachusetts, philanthropist; 4) W.W. Corcoran of Washington, philanthropist, donor of the Corcoran Gallery; 5) Judge James Lyons of Richmond, Va., lawyer, member of the House of Representatives in the First Confederate Congress., 1862-4. All subjects standing are Confederate Generals. Commencing from the left, 1) General James Conner of South Carolina, attorney general of that State under Wade Hampton; 2) General Martin W. Gary of South Carolina; 3) Major General J. Bankhead Magruder of Virginia; 4) General Robert D. Lilley of Virginia; 5) General Beauregard of Louisiana; 6) General Alexander R. Lawton of Georgia; 7) General Henry A. Wise of Virginia, Governor of Virginia during the period of John Brown's raid;)8 General Joseph L. Brent of Maryland, who died in 1905, last survivor of all Americans in the photograph.

The Greenbrier

Other People And
Places Of Interest

A view of Charles Town during the Civil War. Date unknown.   HFNHP

The Kanawha River and a Union Army camp, on the south side opposite Charleston, Kanawha County, in 1863. The scene was painted by Margaretta Doddridge from a vantage point near what is now Morris Street. The camp was located just below the present C and O railroad station. The island shown downstream is probably today's Magic Island.   WVU Archives

This house is thought to have been Gen. Jackson's headquarters while he was in Romney.

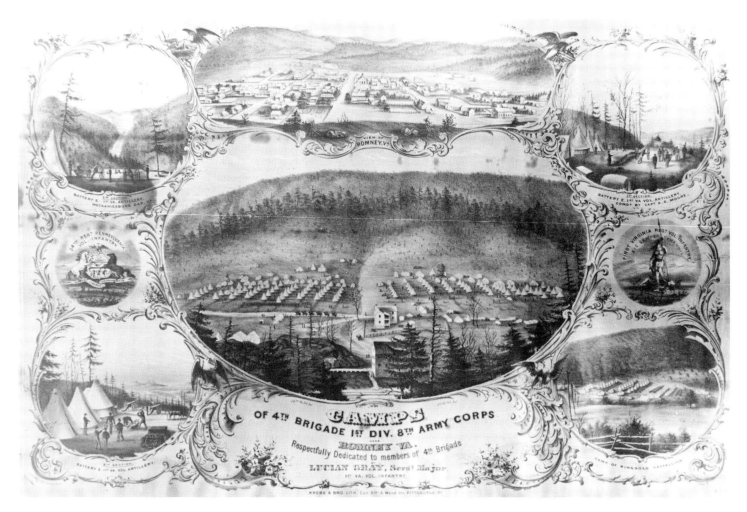

Norma Long, Romney, W. Va.

The Berkeley County Courthouse in Martinsburg, at the corner of King and Queen streets. It was built in 1856. During the war, Union troops destroyed the county records, and Belle Boyd, infamous Confederate spy from Martinsburg, was imprisoned here several times. HPU

MARTINSBURG.

Martinsburg during the war.   Berkeley-Martinsburg Public Library

Buffalo Academy at Buffalo, Putnam County. It was built in 1849 and used as a hospital during the war. Gen. John McCausland attended school here.

Confederate Gen. John McCausland's home in Mason County on Route 35. The general built the house in 1885 and lived here until he died in 1927.

Greenbottom, on State Route 2 near Lesage, Cabell County, the home of Confederate Gen. Albert Jenkins. It was constructed in 1835 and is still occupied. HPU

Boydville, at 601 S. Queen St. in Martinsburg, Berkeley County. It was built in 1800 by Gen. Elisha Boyd and was the home of Gen. Boyd's son-in-law, Charles James Faulkner I, Minister to France in 1860-61, and his son, Charles James Faulkner II, a U.S. Senator from 1887 to 1889. Gen. David Hunter ordered the building burned in 1864, but President Lincoln countermanded the order and the house was saved.
Mr. & Mrs. G.R. Cheesman, Martinsburg, W.Va.

The Craik-Patton House at Daniel Boone Park east of Charleston, Kanawha County, on Route 60. The house was built in 1835 and bought by George Patton in 1858. It has been moved to this site and restored by the Society of Colonial Dames of America.

Thomas Carroll House at 234 Guyan Street, Guyandotte, Cabell County. The house was constructed in 1810 in Gallipolis, Ohio, floated down the Ohio River and rebuilt on its present site in 1810. In 1835, Thomas Carroll used the house as a church and later as a boarding house and inn for rivermen. Mrs. Carroll's pleas saved the house from burning by Federal troops in 1861.

Willow Wall home at Old Fields, Hardy County on Route 220. It was the headquarters of McNeill's Rangers, a Confederate partisan group that operated in the area. The Battle of Moorefield was fought in the vicinity on Aug. 7, 1864.

Hermitage Motor Inn on Route 220 in Petersburg, Grant County. It was built with slave labor in the 1840s and has been in continuous use as an inn since 1881. During the war it housed Federal army officers.

Halfway House at Ansted, Fayette County, on old Route 60. It was built in 1810 and used as the headquarters of the Chicago Grey Dragoons during the winter of 1861-62.

Old Stone House (Tyree Tavern), two miles off Route 60 and one mile off Route 41, on Stonehouse Road near Babcock State Park, Fayette County. It was built in 1824 by Samuel Tyree and was a well-known stagecoach stop on the James River and Kanawha Turnpike. Many famous guests stopped here for the night, and during the war, both sides occupied the house many times.

The Presbyterian Church on Main Street in Moorefield, Hardy County. It was constructed in 1847. Union troops stabled their horses here during the war, and 50 years later the government paid an indemnity for damages incurred. It is still in use today.

Morris Memorial Church in Cedar Grove, Kanawha County, on Route 60. It was built in 1853 on the site of the first church in the Kanawha Valley. During the war it served as a Confederate hospital and as a stable for Union cavalry. After the war the Federal Government paid the church $700 for damages caused by Union soldiers. It has now been restored.

Romney Classical Institute at the north end of Romney, Hampshire County. It was built in 1846 by the Literary Society of Romney and was used by both sides during the war. It is now part of the W. Va. School for the Deaf and Blind.

Weston State Hospital in Lewis County. It was established by the Virginia Assembly in 1858 and construction started the same year. It was first called the Trans-Allegheny Lunatic Asylum but the name was changed to the West Virginia Hospital for the Insane in 1863. Construction continued on the building during the war, but patients were moved to Ohio because of the war-time conditions in the area. In 1864, the asylum was opened and is the largest hand cut stone building in the world.

A Federal cannon in City Park, Parkersburg, Wood County. It was once located at Fort Boreman, a Federal fort built in 1863, guarding the Ohio River at Parkersburg.

Cleante Janutolo Springs at Fayetteville, Fayette County, on Route 21. It was used by both armies during the war.

Organ Cave, five miles south of Caldwell, Greenbrier County, on Route 63. The Confederates made gunpowder here and supposedly held church services inside the cave.

The Dietz Farm at Meadow Bluff, Greenbrier County, off Route 60. This was a major campsite for both armies in this part of the state and was Lee's headquarters in 1861. The house was used as a hospital, and, supposedly, soldiers are buried on a nearby hillside.

The only national cemetery in the state, located in Grafton, Taylor County. It was established in 1868, and 1,200 Civil War soldiers are buried here.

The Jackson family cemetery in Clarksburg, Harrison County, on Route 50. Most of the relatives of Gen. Stonewall Jackson's family are buried here. Jackson's mother is buried in Ansted.

Sweet Springs on Route 3 in Monroe County. This famous old health spa was opened in 1833 and served both armies as a rest stop and staging area. The main building was based on a design by Thomas Jefferson. The resort closed in 1930 and is now the Andrew S. Rowan Memorial Home, a state institution for the aged.

Bath House and Swimming Pool at Sweet Springs. Soldiers no doubt used these facilities during their rest periods.

The main hotel at Salt Sulphur Springs, built about 1820 and now restored. It, too, must have been used extensively during the war.

The Erskine House at Salt Sulphur Springs, Monroe County, built about 1836. This view is from the early 1900s; the building is now in ruins. During the war the old health spa was used as a rest area and head-quarters by both armies, and this building was undoubtedly used as a barracks or hospital.

Site of Fort Pickens at Duffy, Lewis County, two miles east of Ireland on Route 19. Company A, 10th West Virginia Volunteer Infantry, built the fort for their headquarters in 1861-62. It was burned in 1864.

ROOM ACCOMMODATIONS 500.

BATH HOUSES.

CAPON

Site of Fort Pendelton on Maryland side facing Gormania, Grant County, on Route 50. It was used by Federal troops to guard the Northwestern Turnpike. Arrows point to existing trenches.

Capon Springs on Route 16 off Route 259 in Hampshire County. This is a view from the 1860s. The popular resort was in operation prior to 1800, and the hotel, built about 1850 and one of the largest structures in the South, was named "Mountain House." Robert E. Lee and his wife were visiting the spa in 1859 when he was called to Harpers Ferry to put down the attack by John Brown. In 1861, with the war coming and the resort $8,000 in debt, the state ordered the place sold, However, the new state of West Virginia took it over, and Capon Springs became part of the debt that West Virginia owed Virginia after the war.   Virginia Tech Archives

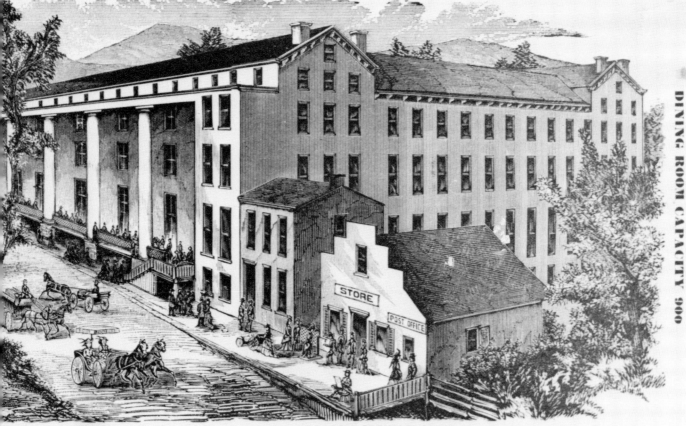

NGS.   CAPON SPRINGS HOTEL.

The old pier of the covered bridge over the Tygart River at Fetterman (Grafton), Taylor County on Route 50. It was built in 1834-35 on the Northwestern Turnpike and destroyed by a flood in 1888.

The Mud River Bridge at Milton, Cabell County. Milton was a small settlement on the James River and Kanawha Turnpike established in the 1830s. On April 5, 1863, Confederates under Capt. Carpenter tried to take the bridge but were repulsed. This bridge was probably built in the 1870s to replace the one at the site during the war.

HPU

Two views of Fort Mullegan at Petersburg, Grant County, on Route 28. It was constructed by the Union Army and is one of the best preserved Civil War forts in the state. Extensive breastworks and trenches are still visible.

Civil War trenches at Belington, Barbour County.

A common grave for 95 Confederate soldiers who were killed in the Lewisburg vicinity. The grave, which overlooks the town is shaped in the form of a cross.

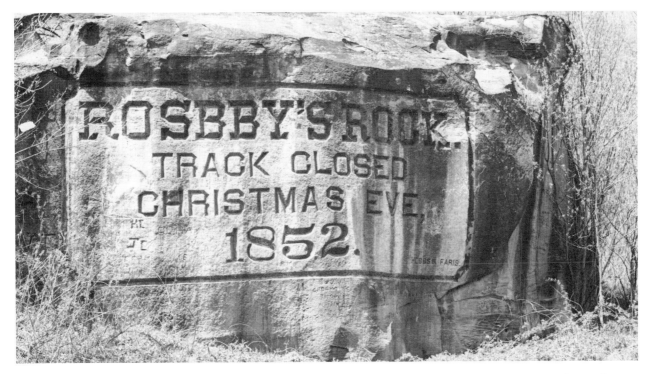

Rosbby's Rock on Big Grave Creek Road, six miles east of Moundsville, Marshall County. The rock commemorates the completion of the Baltimore and Ohio Railroad to Wheeling in 1852.

Glen Ferris Inn, Fayette County, on Route 60. It was built in 1816 and was a major stopping point on the James River and Kanawha Turnpike prior to the Civil War. Thousands of troops passed by here during the early part of the war.

Col. Lewis Wallace of the 11th Indiana Volunteers (Zouave Regiment) and his staff in West Virginia. Wallace would be known after the war for his famous novel Ben Hur.

West Virginia Hillbilly

A wartime scene at Buffalo, Putnam County, showing elements of the 7th West Virginia Regiment of U.S. Volunteers.　　Terry Lowry

Jackson's Mill, Lewis County in the late 1800s. This was the boyhood home of the famous Confederate general T.J. (Stonewall) Jackson who was born at Clarksburg in 1824.   WVU Archives

Jackson's Mill just off Route 19 near Weston. The mill was built in 1837. Arrow points to location of the home Jackson lived in. The site is now owned and operated by West Virginia University and is the state 4-H camp.

McMurran Hall on King Street in Shepherds-town, Jefferson County. It was built in 1859-60 to be used as the town hall and library but was used as a hospital during the war. It served as the Jefferson County Courthouse from 1866 to 1871, at which time the county seat was relocated to Charles Town. It is now part of Shepherd College. Shepherd College

Close-up view of Jackson's home at Jackson's Mill. Author's Collection

Gen. David Hunter Strother (1816-88) was born in Martinsburg, Berkeley County. He was a general in the Union army and fought in Virginia and Louisiana and with his cousin Gen. David Hunter in the 1864 Virginia Valley campaign. He was well known during and after the war as a correspondent and artist for Harpers Weekly magazine, using the pen name "Porte Crayon."

W.Va. State Archives

Gen. Jesse Lee Reno (1823-62) was born in Wheeling, Ohio County. He was the highest ranking Union officer from the state and was killed at the Battle of South Mountain in September, 1862.   W.Va. State Archives

General Jesse Lee Reno

Billy Crump of Co. I, 23rd Ohio Infantry. He was an orderly to Col. Rutherford B. Hayes when he was stationed at Gauley Bridge in February 1863. He is shown on Hayes' horse, which he borrowed, along with his pistol. He set off from camp and traveled 20 miles to forage for supplies.   USAMHI

Nancy Hart, of Roane County, who fought with the Moccasin Rangers, a Confederate partisan group operating in central West Virginia. She was arrested as a spy and housed in the jail at Summersville. She was permitted to go about the grounds of the jail, and a careless guard allowed her to handle his gun. Without any warning she killed the guard and escaped. She led Confederate troops back to Summersville where they drove the Union forces from the town. After the war she married a former Ranger and lived in Greenbrier County until her death in 1902.   W.Va. State Archives

Ruffner Park on Kanawha Boulevard in Charleston. The monument was erected to the Kanawha Riflemen, a local military group that entered Confederate service.

The 23rd Ohio Volunteer Infantry band at Charleston in 1863.   RBHL

In 1866 the Confederate Memorial Association was organized in Romney to erect a monument to the soldiers of Hampshire County. Money was raised by sewing bees and fairs and the monument was ordered in 1867 from Baltimore. But feelings about the war were still very intense. Because of a fear that Federal sympathizers would destroy the monument, the inscription was left off until the last moment before it was boxed up and shipped hurriedly to Romney. It was dedicated on Sept. 26, 1867 and is thought to be the first monument erected to Confederate dead.

Monument at the Valley Mountain campsite of Gen. Lee's command in 1861. It was erected in 1901 near Mace, Pocahontas County.

Jack Zinn, Nutter Fort, W. Va.

Monument to Confederate dead next to the Greenbrier County Library, Lewisburg.

CONFEDERATE SOLDIERS
OF
MONROE COUNTY

Monument to the Confederate soldiers of Monroe County. It was erected in a field on the edge of Union in 1901.

Monument to native son, Gen. Stonewall Jackson, in front of the Harrison County Court-house in Clarksburg. State of West Virginia

THOMAS
"STONEWALL"
JACKSON

The Battle of Philippi was re-enacted on its 100th anniversary in 1961.

A re-enactment of the Battle of Droop Mountain took place on Labor Day, 1974.   State of West Virginia

Bibliography

Ambler, Charles H., *West Virginia, The Mountain State*, Prentice-Hall, New York, 1940.

_____, *West Virginia, Stories and Biographies*, Rand McNally & Co., New York, 1937.

Auvil, Myrtle, *Covered Bridges of West Virginia*, McClain Printing Co., Parsons, W.Va., 1972.

Blackwell, Lyle, *Gauley Bridge, The Town and its First Church*, The Gauley Bridge Baptist Church, 1960.

Boatner, Mark Mayo, *The Civil War Dictionary*, D. McKay Co., New York, 1959.

Calhoun, Harrison Mayberry, *'Twixt North and South,'* McCoy Publishing Co., Franklin, W.Va., 1974.

Cometti, Elizabeth and Summers, Festus P., *The 35th State, A Documentary History of West Virginia*, McClain Printing Co., Parsons, W.Va., 1966.

Conley, Phil and Doherty, William Thomas, *West Virginia History*, Education Foundation, Inc., Charleston, W.Va., 1974.

Cook, Roy Bird, *Lewis County in the Civil War, 1861-65*, Jarrett Printing Co., Charleston, W.Va., 1924.

Donnelly, Shirley, *Miscellaneous Historical Notes on Fayette County, W.Va.*, 1958.

Duffey, J.W., *Two Generals Kidnapped*, Moorfield Examiner, Moorefield, W.Va., 1944.

Hendricks, Sam, *Military Operations in Jefferson County, Va. (and W.Va.)*, Shepherdstown, W.Va., 1910.

Hornbeck, Betty, *Upshur Brothers of the Blue and Gray*, McClain Printing Co., Parsons, W.Va., 1967.

Humphreys, Milton W., *Military Operations; 1861-63, Fayette County, W.Va.*, Charles Goodard.

Lowry, Terry, *The Battle of Scary Creek, Military Operations in the Kanawha Valley, April-July 1861*, Pictorial Histories Publishing Co., Charleston, W.Va., 1982.

_____, *September Blood, The Battle of Carnifex Ferry*, Pictorial Histories Publishing Co., Charleston, W.Va., 1985.

McCormick, Kyle, *A Story of the Formation of West Virginia*, W.Va. Dept. of Archives and History, Charleston, W.Va., 1961.

_____, *The New River—Kanawha River and the Mine War of West Virginia*, Matthews Printing Co., Charleston, W.Va., 1959.

_____, *The Story of Mercer County*, Charleston Printing Co., 1957.

Moore, George E., *A Banner in the Hills; West Virginia's Statehood*, Appleton-Century-Crofts, New York, 1963.

Rice, Otis, *Charleston and the Kanawha Valley*, Windsor Publications, Woodland Hills, Calif., 1981.

Selected Archeological and Historical Sites in West Virginia, Preliminary Plan for Development, Wheeling College, 1965.

Shiney, Mervin, *The Big Sewell Mountain Country, A Short History*, Nuttall High School, 1934.

Stutler, Boyd B., *West Virginia in the Civil War*, Education Foundation Inc., Charleston, W.Va., 1963.

Summers, Festus P., *The Baltimore and Ohio in the Civil War*, G.P. Putnam, New York, 1939.

Williams, Thomas Harry, *Hayes of the 23rd; the Civil War Volunteer Officer*, Alfred Knopf, New York, 1965.

Writer Program WPA, *West Virginia—A Guide to the Mountain State*, Oxford University Press, New York, 1941.

Zinn, Jack, *The Battle of Rich Mountain*, McClain Printing Co., Parsons, W.Va., 1974.

_____, *R.E. Lee's Cheat Mountain Campaign*, McClain Printing Co., Parsons, W.Va., 1974.

Plus many newspaper articles, county histories, historical society publications, pamphlets, the *West Virginia Review* Magazine, the *West Virginia History* Magazine and general Civil War history books.

Index

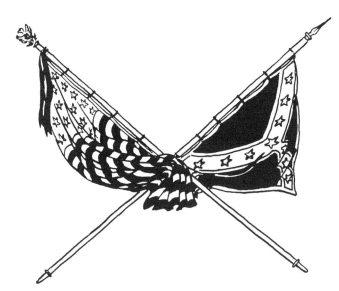